"The world faces a number of monumental challenges, ranging from persistent inequality and the aging of the population to climate change and the rise of the robot. In this innovative, accessible, and persuasive book, Maxton and Randers show that we don't need revolutionary changes to meet these challenges. They tell us how big changes can be—indeed, can only be—achieved through a set of reforms that are moderate enough to be politically feasible in the short run. It is an essential guide to those who want to change the world for the better—and for certain."

HA-JOON CHANG, Faculty of Economics, University of Cambridge, author of *23 Things They Don't Tell You about Capitalism* and *Economics: The User's Guide*

"A fascinating, data-rich look at some of the most fundamental questions our species has ever faced—and a striking argument for maturity over endless growth."

BILL MCKIBBEN, author of *Deep Economy*

"Do you want a cogent and accessible explanation of why our paramount policy goal of GDP growth is increasing unemployment, inequality, and environmental destruction—while reducing welfare? Then read this informative book for both answers and better policies!"

HERMAN DALY, emeritus professor, University of Maryland

"The problems society faces to achieve a sustainable and desirable future are well known, but solutions seem impossible. Maxton and Randers describe thirteen politically feasible proposals that can actually solve these problems. A must-read for anyone who wants to create a better world."

PROF. ROBERT COSTANZA, VC's chair in public policy, Crawford School of Public Policy, Australian National University

"This book has the power to induce policy changes that are imperative for the creation of an equitable, peaceful, and sustainable future for human society."

RAJENDRA K. PACHAURI, past-chair, Intergovernmental Panel on Climate Change (IPCC); executive vice chairman, The Energy and Resources Institute (TERI)

"*Reinventing Prosperity,* appearing nearly forty-five years after *The Limits to Growth,* is another wake-up call of historic significance. It reinforces the important messages of Laudato Si', the UN Sustainable Development Goals, and the Paris Climate Agreement. I endorse these proposals for another economy that is both more fair and more sustainable."

RUUD LUBBERS, co-founder of the Earth Charter   .

"Maxton and Rander's groundbreaking book gets us thirteen steps closer to the carbon-free economy by 2050."

MATHIS WACKERNAGEL, PhD, founder and CEO, Global Footprint Network

"Maxton and Randers present a new path toward sustainability by focusing on a set of measures that should be more readily acceptable, because they provide short-term advantages to the majority of people. *Reinventing Prosperity* is a compelling book, full of new insights and iconoclastic ideas."

ROBERTO PECCEI, vice chancellor for research emeritus, UCLA

"Maxton and Randers bring a rare combination of insight, pragmatism, and a global perspective to the challenge of managing economies in the twenty-first century. Their thirteen policy proposals should be taken seriously by anyone who believes that thoughtful, informed, democratic change offers the best chance for a prosperous future."

PETER A. VICTOR, PhD, FRSC, author of *Managing without Growth: Slower by Design, not Disaster*

REINVENTING PROSPERITY

Foreword by David Suzuki

GRAEME MAXTON & JORGEN RANDERS

REINVENTING

PROSPERITY

Managing Economic Growth to Reduce Unemployment, Inequality, and Climate Change

A Report to the Club of Rome

DAVID SUZUKI INSTITUTE

GREYSTONE BOOKS

Vancouver/Berkeley

16 17 18 19 20   5 4 3 2 1

Greystone Books Ltd.
www.greystonebooks.com

David Suzuki Institute
219–2211 West 4th Avenue
Vancouver BC Canada V6K 4S2

Cataloguing data available from Library and Archives Canada
ISBN 978-1-77164-251-4 (cloth)
ISBN 978-1-77164-252-1 (epub)

Editing by Lesley Cameron
Copy editing by Shirarose Wilensky
Jacket and text design by Nayeli Jimenez
Cartoons by Øystein Runde

Printed and bound in Canada on ancient-forest-friendly paper by Friesens

We gratefully acknowledge the financial support of the British Columbia
Arts Council, the Province of British Columbia through the Book Publishing
Tax Credit, and the Government of Canada for our publishing activities.

Canadä

BRITISH
COLUMBIA

BRITISH COLUMBIA
ARTS COUNCIL
An agency of the Province of British Columbia

Canada Council   Conseil des arts
for the Arts   du Canada

— CONTENTS —

— LIST OF BOXES —

What is green growth? *144*

What does it mean to run out of resources? *145*

Is it possible to pay a guaranteed income to all citizens in a modern society? And if so, how high could that income be? *167*

What human development indicators are currently measured, and what new ones should be added for a smooth transition to a better world? *172*

What does it mean to shift from extreme free-market thinking to modified market thinking? *210*

— LIST OF GRAPHS —

— LIST OF TABLES —

— FOREWORD —

──────────

I WAS INVOLVED IN a battle over logging in a B.C. forest when I met the CEO of the company that had the license to log it. We had a heated argument until he finally yelled, "Listen, Suzuki, are tree huggers like you willing to pay for those trees? Because if you are not, they don't have any value until someone cuts them down." I was dumbfounded, because to me it seemed crazy to let "value" be defined by the economy. But even more overwhelming was my realization that in the current globalized world, he was right.

The CEO could give me chapter and verse on the volume of pulp, board feet of lumber, jobs that would be created, and profit for his company, while I was left sputtering that berries could be picked and sold, salal gathered for flower arrangements, ecotourism opportunities found, and maybe a cure for cancer discovered.

But the real reason we were fighting to protect the forest from logging was that all the plants and trees were removing carbon from the atmosphere and replacing it with oxygen, not a bad service for animals like us that can't exist without photosynthesis, yet economists dismiss it as an "externality," irrelevant in an economic equation. The forest pumps vast quantities of water out of the soil, transpires it into the air, and modulates weather and climate—another externality. The tree roots cling to soil and prevent erosion onto salmon spawning grounds—externality. The intact forest provides habitat for countless species of insects, microorganisms, amphibians, mammals, and birds—all externalities. What kind of economic system ignores the very things that keep the biosphere habitable for animals like us?

To top off what I think is a ludicrous system is the endless economic growth that is the goal of politicians and corporate leaders. Ask a corporate CEO or political leader how well they did last year and within a microsecond, they will refer to growth in GDP, profit, or jobs as the definition of success or failure. But steady growth forever is the goal of cancer cells, and by emulating that creed, economists doom us to the same end—death. Nothing within a finite world like the biosphere can grow forever, and the attempt to maintain constant growth is the cause of the current wave of species extinction.

As Graeme Maxton and Jorgen Randers explain in *Reinventing Prosperity*, we need to radically overhaul the current globalized economic system by asking important questions that have been ignored for too long: What is an economy for? What is prosperity? Are there no limits? How much is enough? Are we happier with all the stuff generated in the current economy?

The very word "economy" has the same roots as "ecology," namely the Greek word "*oikos*," meaning household or domain. Ecology is the study of our home to determine the laws and principles that govern a species' survival, whereas economics is the management of that domain. But when politicians suggest that the cost of reducing greenhouse gases to limit climate change will "destroy the economy," we elevate that economy above the very atmosphere that keeps us healthy and alive.

Instead of being bogged down by arguments about jobs, corporate profits, GDP, and the national economy, we first have to establish an indisputable "bottom line" on which all sectors of society can agree. So let me make a stab at it. We live in a world that is shaped and constrained by immutable laws of nature that we accept and live with.

Physics informs us that we cannot build a rocket that will travel faster than the speed of light, create an antigravity vehicle on Earth, or make a perpetual motion machine. Only science-fiction writers speculate on surpassing the dictates of physics. Chemistry, too, imposes limits through the atomic properties of the elements, reaction rates, and diffusion constants, so we know what can or cannot be synthesized in a lab. And biology also shapes our lives. The maximum number of a plant or animal species is dictated by the carrying capacity of an ecosystem or habitat. Exceed that number and the population will crash. Because of our intelligence, we are able to adapt to a wide array of ecosystems, from deserts to Arctic tundra, tropical rain forests, and prairies, but the biosphere itself imposes a carrying capacity on our species. For us, the maximum sustainable population will be dictated by both numbers and per capita consumption. So the industrialized world, by virtue of its hyperconsumption, is vastly overpopulated, and most scientists agree that the collective impact of our species far exceeds the planet's capacity to sustain it.

Human beings are animals, and as biological creatures, we have an absolute need for clean air, water, soil, and food; photosynthesis; and biodiversity. Deprived of air for four minutes, we die; forced to breathe polluted air, we sicken. So protection of clean air should be a top priority in any human-made system. After six to seven days without water, we die; contaminated water makes us sick. So clean water must also be a priority of the highest order. We can survive four to six weeks without food before succumbing, and contaminated food makes us sick. So clean food and soil on which it's grown is a chief priority. Every bit of the energy in our bodies that we need to grow, move, and reproduce is sunlight captured by plants in photosynthesis and converted to chemical energy. Then we get that energy by eating plants, or animals that eat the plants. When we need that energy, we burn it to liberate the sun's energy in our bodies.

Finally, the miracle of life on Earth is that the four fundamental elements of life—clean air, water, soil, and photosynthesis—are provided to us by the web of life on the planet. Plants create the oxygen-rich, carbon dioxide-poor atmosphere; soil fungi, microorganisms, and plant roots filter water to make it potable as it percolates through earth; life is both all of our food and the creator of soil on which to grow it; and finally, all of the fuel we use, from wood to peat, dung, coal, oil, and gas, was created by life.

So I believe whatever political and economic systems we create should rest on the foundation that makes life possible: clean air, clean water, clean soil and food, photosynthesis, and biodiversity. Protecting those elements must be the highest priority of all people and their systems, because they determine our very survival and well-being and are defined by laws of nature that we can't change.

Other things such as the borders we draw around property, cities, provinces, states, and nations do not emerge from nature, and nature pays no attention to them. Think of air, water, even eroding soil—they do not heed the boundaries we kill and die for.

Capitalism, the economy, markets, and corporations are not forces of nature; we invented them. We cannot shoehorn nature into the demands and constrictions of our creations, because we can't alter the laws that govern the real world. The only things we can change are those that we created, yet we act as if the demands of the economy or the market must dictate the way we act.

Reinventing Prosperity provides a way of seeing past the demands of an unsustainable and destructive system, beginning with a new definition of prosperity that makes sense in our lives. Maxton and Randers chart a persuasive and feasible path into a future that offers greater happiness, equity, and meaning, and a rich environment.

DAVID SUZUKI

THERE ARE MANY things to be concerned about in the world, from persistently high levels of unemployment and widening inequality to continued resource depletion, rising pollution, increasing biodiversity losses, and widespread poverty.

The biggest problem, however, is the gradual change humanity is causing to the climate. If nothing is done to stop global warming, progress in almost all areas of human endeavor will gradually slow over the next fifty years because of more frequent, and more scary, climatic events—and worse will follow.

Unfortunately, almost nothing is currently being done to address this problem.

People do not respond because they do not dare to challenge the existing economic system, because they believe that the steps needed to cut greenhouse gas emissions will reduce economic growth. They think that lower economic growth will increase joblessness in the rich world and condemn much of the poor world to decades of poverty, which in turn will increase inequality—a big enough problem already. So, rather than making the transition to a cleaner, more sustainable world, people focus on boosting economic growth because they believe this will increase the number of jobs and improve living standards, even though inequalities have been widening and the climate problem is worsening. Once there are more jobs and people are better off, they seem to be saying, society can take the steps needed to fix the climate problem.

If we could show that it is possible to overcome this hurdle, we reasoned, if we could break the perceived link between economic growth, jobs, and equality, we might change this. If we could show that it is possible to create jobs, boost average living standards, and reduce inequality—even without any economic growth at all—we could overcome the major barrier that stops people from acting.

That is what this book is about. It is about how to cut unemployment and narrow the gap between rich and poor in the developed world while slowing the pace of climate change. It is about how to make sure that everyone has enough paid work, or enough income, to live comfortably. It is about how to make the transition to a cleaner, greener world without making people worse off in the process.

Many of our recommendations are unconventional, and some will certainly be controversial. Because they frequently run against the current political and economic tide, the knee-jerk reaction may be to reject them. They often require a little time for reflection before people can see that they really do describe a better path forward, a viable way to increase average living standards everywhere.

To help the reader understand the intellectual basis of our book, we have included a number of boxes in the text with extra information in the form of a short answer to a question that inquisitive readers are likely to be asking themselves.

We have sought to place the boxes on the page where you are likely to ask the question first. But you might also want to use the list of boxes on page vii to navigate as questions spring to mind.

We have already said that many of the ideas we present in this book would increase average well-being, or living standards, in the rich world. One of the main obstacles to this is what we call "extreme free-market thinking" (see Box: What is "extreme free-market thinking"?).

What is "extreme free-market thinking"?

Extreme free-market thinking is the sort of thinking that seeks individual consumption growth, promotes competition and free trade, views collective action as inefficient, and sees high taxes

---

and strong government as dangerous. It promotes the idea that raising output (GDP) is more important than raising the output per person (GDP per inhabitant). It argues that the best way to increase well-being is through boosting GDP, downplaying the fact that this often serves the interests of the rich more than the poor. Finally, it enforces short-term thinking by using high interest rates to discount the future costs and benefits of human activities (for an explanation of this see Box: What is short-termism?).

We are painfully aware that extreme free-market thinking is fully, or at the very least partly, embraced by most of the rich world's citizens, who are more interested in boosting short-term consumption than the well-being of current and future generations. We see this short-termism as another significant obstacle that needs to be overcome (see Box: What is short-termism?).

What is short-termism?

Short-termism is the tendency to place more emphasis on the short-term consequences of a decision—on what it might mean for people over the coming hours, weeks, or years—than on the long-term consequences—on what it might mean over the coming decades, possibly even beyond the lifetime of current generations.

In economic theory, and often in the practical world of business and government, people generally choose the outcome that offers the highest net present value (NPV). The NPV is the sum of all the future costs and benefits of a decision discounted to their value today. It recognizes that a benefit in the future is worth less than it is today. That is, $10,000 today is better than $10,000 in a year's time. This is because you could invest the $10,000 you have today in a business or put it in the bank and earn interest. If you could earn 10% a year, then you would have $11,000 in a year. (To keep things simple, we are excluding the effect of inflation.)

Economists in both business and government calculate the NPV using something called the "discount rate." When it comes to big decisions, such as building a new airport, this is usually set quite high—at around 10% a year—partly because there are many other competing uses for these funds.

To find the total NPV of a project, they add up the discounted net income (revenue minus the costs) from each year, and if the cost of building the airport today is less than the total discounted revenue made over the life of the project, it has a positive NPV and is deemed "profitable." Conventional economics says it therefore makes sense to make the investment and build the airport.

This approach has several troubling consequences, however. It means that the benefits that accrue more than thirty years into the future have very little value at all, and the further ahead they lie, the lower they are valued today. This is because the further any benefit lies into the future, the more heavily it is discounted, so the less it appears to be worth.

This means that costs in the future have almost no value either. If people do something today that will damage the environment in fifty years, then that cost is valued at almost zero today. With a 10% discount rate, $1 million of damage in fifty years has a consequence that is valued at just $9,400 today, according to this sort of financial thinking.

The use of these high discount rates is one of the main reasons why most of the actions needed to stop climate change are so difficult to implement when the alternatives are to create more economic growth or do nothing.

If we had some magical power, we would end this short-termism in markets, politics, and the population at large. Sadly, we do not have magical powers. But we do have extensive knowledge of economics, climate science, and human development. So we have restricted ourselves to thirteen proposals that could not only create a better world but also offer immediate benefits to the majority of people. We have, in other words, only offered proposals that should be politically feasible in societies with a short-termist view of the world.

We wish you good reading, and hope that you might find something in what we write that will inspire you to help build a better world.

GPM AND JR
Europe, August 30, 2016

Please note: The views expressed in this book are those of the authors, and although they are shared by many of our colleagues in the Club of Rome, they do not represent the views of the club.

CHAPTER I

TWO URGENT PROBLEMS
IN THE RICH WORLD

Two of the most urgent problems facing the modern rich world
are persistent unemployment and rising inequality.

IN THE RICH world, the gap between rich and poor has been widening.[1] As there has been strong economic growth for most of the last thirty years, this is something of a puzzle. Economic growth was meant to reduce inequality. The trickle-down effect, where the spending by the rich descends through some sort of economic filtration into the pockets of the poor, should have fortified the general population and raised living standards for everyone.

Yet millions of people in the rich world today live in conditions more like those of Victorian Britain. In the United States, 49 million people—out of a total population of 320 million—live in poverty.[2] In Europe, it is one in every seven.[3] In Eastern Europe, Spain, and Greece, poverty affects one in five, with women, single-parent families, and the young worst affected. Including those on very low incomes, a quarter of the population of the developed—rich—world is currently classified as being "at risk of poverty or exclusion." That is almost 200 million people.

As the gap between rich and poor has widened, unemployment has also risen throughout the rich world, and it remains stubbornly high. Particularly badly afflicted are those under the age of twenty-five, though millions of baby-boomers in their fifties and sixties have found themselves without any income, pension, or work prospects too. And there has been a huge increase in the number of under-employed, those who want to work more but cannot find a paid full-time job.

At a time of record global wealth, and after so many decades of healthy economic growth, none of this should be. For decades, economists told people that economic growth would bring jobs, better incomes, and higher standards of living. But it has not.

What on earth is going on?

British charity Oxfam puts it simply. There has been a "power grab"[4] by the rich, it says.[5] It accuses the world's fattest fat cats of manipulating the political system to rig the rules of the game in their favor, so that they are taxed less, regulated less, and scrutinized less. As a result, wealth and income have been moving in the opposite direction from what people believed.

Without change, this situation will not improve. The rich will continue to get richer because, as we will explain, that is what the current economic system does. Proponents of today's free-market model like to claim that it promotes a more egalitarian society. In reality, though, as we will show, it has created a society that is more like a gigantic casino where the outcome is rigged in favor of the rich.

In his groundbreaking book *Capital in the Twenty-First Century*, French economist Thomas Piketty predicts that if nothing changes, much of the developed world will gradually return to something more like the nineteenth century, to a time when factory owners, entrepreneurs, and bankers controlled most of the wealth and everyone else struggled to survive. He sees a future in which the rich world's middle classes effectively disappear.

This raises a fundamental and troubling question. Were the few decades after World War II, when the gap between rich and poor greatly declined, an anomaly caused by a particular set of circumstances? Is it possible that the natural order is more like the world of the past, more like that which reigned for most of human history, where a tiny minority controlled almost all the wealth and the vast majority were very poor?

It is an increasingly difficult question to answer. For most of the last seventy years, a rich world dominated by a middle class has seemed so natural and so right. Yet, historically, it is an oddity. At no other time in the last two thousand years has a middle class existed on such a scale.

Unless there is a radical shift in economic direction, Piketty says, "the past will devour the future," and the few decades of comparative comfort enjoyed by the middle classes during the second half of the twentieth century will be consigned to the history books as little more than an interesting, but temporary, social phenomenon.

Piketty's solution is a global wealth tax. He believes that there should be much greater cooperation between national tax authorities to exchange and share data on individual wealth, as well as a more "equitable tax system" for governments to invest in infrastructure and education. Taxation should be used to redistribute wealth and create a more balanced society, he says.

This will be difficult to implement, though, because it would require the rich world's politicians to do the opposite of what they have done for the last thirty years: to tax their biggest financial supporters and most powerful citizens more.

Other economists have suggested that the inequality and unemployment problems should be tackled by boosting infrastructure spending, to create jobs; by changing intellectual property rights, to create more opportunities for people to access new technologies and ideas; and by changing the education system, to encourage more entrepreneurs.

None of these solutions addresses the underlying problem, however. Offering large numbers of people the chance to work—to build new roads or tunnels or to set themselves up in business, for example—gives them work and the opportunity to earn an income. But it does not change a system in which wealth gradually flows from the majority to the rich, as we will explain.

Such proposals offer only a temporary fix, helping the poor to earn more and the unemployed to find some work, without offering long-term change.

We believe the solution needs to be more radical. Rich-world nations will need to change their economic systems. They will need to step back from today's economic mantra, which promotes individual freedom, applauds free markets and free trade, and minimizes state influence, and instead rearrange their economies to boost average well-being. Markets and trade should not be left largely unregulated any longer but actively managed. Governments should also be "right sized"—that is, small enough to ensure that they operate efficiently but big enough to be able to do their job well and tackle the challenges that lie ahead.

There is one other problem, however. The current economic system also requires continuous growth in the throughput of natural resources to function. This is built into the system's DNA. People need to consume ever more, and manufacturers need to produce ever more to stop unemployment rising and keep the system functioning.

The trouble is, this process is generating ever-greater quantities of greenhouse gases, and these are causing the climate of the planet to change. This has already become so bad that global weather patterns will continue to worsen for decades and sea levels will rise, regardless of what is done now.

Yet any attempt to manage economic growth, and so slow down the environmental damage, shuts off the fuel that keeps the economic engine running. A slowing economy increases unemployment, as well as inequality and poverty, even more.

The current economic system has put the developed world on a treadmill that is driving society in a hopeless social and environmental direction, yet any conventional attempt to stop what is happening only makes the situation worse.

Conventional solutions cannot reduce inequality and joblessness (or climate change). Nor will a wealth tax, boosting infrastructure spending, or encouraging more entrepreneurs.

What are needed are unconventional solutions that will be attractive to the majority of people, so that they will welcome the transition.

The proposals in this book do this. They boost average well-being while at the same time cutting unemployment and reducing inequality, while offering an immediate benefit to the majority. That they also happen to reduce the rate of climate change (though not fix it) might be incidental to many readers. But it is not incidental to us. It is the reason we wrote this book.

CHAPTER 2

THE TRADITIONAL SOLUTION:
ECONOMIC GROWTH

*Traditionally, economic growth has been seen as the best
way to reduce unemployment and inequality.*

ALMOST NO MATTER where you live in the world, economic growth has become something of a constant. For more than thirty years, businesspeople, governments, and politicians have seen the pursuit of economic growth as their main goal. News reports and commentators focus on it endlessly. Taxi drivers, bankers, and economists often seem to talk of little else: How is it possible to boost economic growth? Why is the growth rate down this quarter? When will the economy recover?

Economic growth appears to be in our collective blood. It is hard to believe that it was not always so.

What is economic growth?

It is regrettable that the word "growth" is often used alone in the context of the economy, because this leads to much unnecessary confusion in the world. It is always necessary to be precise and to explain exactly what is growing, whether it is the economy (the total gross domestic product, otherwise known as GDP), demand, consumption, or GDP per person, for example. The descriptor matters because these variables do not move in parallel. If consumption grows, for example, that does not necessarily mean that the economy also grows. More importantly, it matters because these variables do not contribute equally to human well-being.

If you want to be a source of clear thinking never use the word "growth" alone. Explain what is growing!

Economic growth is the increase in the total output of an economy from one period to another, typically measured in percent per year. The total output is the market value of all goods and services produced in a nation in a set time period, less the costs of the inputs (such as raw materials) used (with an adjustment for trade). The resulting figure is called the gross domestic product. GDP measures the value added in the country in a time period of interest. Economic growth is the same as growth in GDP.

Since most (between two thirds and three quarters) of the output of rich nations is consumer goods and services, economic growth is normally associated with consumption growth—not least because the media often wrongly portrays economic growth and consumption growth as the same thing. But it is not always like this. In times of war, for example, GDP often grows spectacularly because of increased production of military equipment, while consumption declines.

Many people forget that GDP is a measure of the level of activity in an economy, not the level of happiness or the standard of living. GDP certainly increases when more consumer goods and services are produced, but it also increases when prisons are built, when warships are launched and guns are fired, when road accident victims are treated, and when dikes are rebuilt after flood damage.

One particularly important example of an activity that boosts GDP but does not improve well-being is the repair and adaptation work needed in response to climate change.

When GDP rises, there is economic growth. Higher GDP normally requires more labor, which means more jobs and more wages. This means people have more money to spend, leading to higher consumption. The owners of businesses make higher profits, and stock markets tend to rise. More tax is paid, so governments can build new roads and more schools. The economy is running along nicely, in other words.

If the economic engine coughs, and GDP falls, it is usually a sign that something needs to change. Some sectors of the economy have expanded too rapidly perhaps, or people have borrowed too much, or house prices have risen too fast, or companies have failed to invest in new technologies and become uncompetitive.

On such occasions, governments sometimes choose to step in. They might lower interest rates to make it more attractive for investors to initiate new projects or put interest rates up to dampen the housing market. They might offer support to local industries to help them become competitive again.

Or they might do nothing at all.

A modern market economy is, after all, largely self-correcting, thanks to Scottish moral philosopher and historian Adam Smith's famous invisible hand.[1] If house prices are too high, they will eventually drop back to more sensible levels by themselves. If people have borrowed too much, they will eventually start paying back what they owe or declare themselves bankrupt. If businesses become hopelessly uncompetitive, they will go bust.

The good, "up" part of the economic cycle leads to rising production and investment. This brings greater profits, higher tax revenues, rising stock markets, and more jobs. More jobs lead to more consumption.

The bad, "down" part of the cycle works the other way. When people have too many debts, they cut back on their spending and start paying back their loans. Because they buy less, inventories become too full, so factories cut production. Business profits decline and investment falls. Stock markets fall back, unemployment rises, and tax revenues shrink. The downwards spiral continues like this, sometimes for years, until the imbalance that caused the slowdown has been addressed and the system is back near the starting point.

But once there, the cycle restarts and growth resumes. Typically, this cycle repeats itself every four to eight years.

To understand what is happening in their economies, societies track GDP, and so the output of goods and services has become the principal measure of social development. But GDP was never intended to be a measure of well-being. Simon Kuznets, who was the chief architect of the United States' national accounting system and developed the idea of measuring GDP in 1934, cautioned against using it as an indicator of general progress. It was developed for Roosevelt's government to demonstrate that the U.S. economy could provide enough war supplies and still maintain a healthy output of goods and services for consumers. Increasing GDP was never meant to be a goal for modern societies.

In recent decades, GDP has become increasingly important and most people assume that almost all economic growth is good. Growth is not just necessary, they believe, but essential. They assume that increased output leads to higher living standards. This is because they have also been told that there is a trickle-down effect, that the riches created through increased production spread throughout society, narrowing the gap between rich and poor. And they have been told that faster economic growth will create more jobs and reduce unemployment. Because people assume it does all this, GDP has become almost divine. The belief that society should pursue economic growth at all costs is not only assumed to be true, but the underlying assumptions about what it achieves are also rarely questioned.

As we will show, these assumptions were (mostly) correct between 1950 and the early 1980s, but things have changed since then. The pursuit of increased output has actually widened inequality and led to higher levels of unemployment while damaging the environment. It has also increased the number of people living in poverty in much of the developing world.

We will explain how and why this has happened in the coming chapters. For now, however, we will look at one of the first assumptions that people need to ditch to understand what is going on: the idea that economic growth is always good.

Why do most people believe that economic growth is good?

People believe that economic growth is good because it has historically led to rising incomes, higher employment, and safer pensions for most people.

Economic growth certainly has many benefits. But it is not always socially advantageous. What society counts as economic growth is frequently very damaging, whereas what it fails to count, and subsequently ignores, is often vitally important.

When someone builds a house, this generates economic growth—an increase in GDP. If the house falls down because it is badly built, however, the loss is ignored because the collapse did not require any human effort, equipment, or resources. It does not reduce GDP. But building it or deliberately knocking it down adds to GDP because both require labor and equipment.

It may seem counterintuitive, but gigantic storms, such as Hurricane Sandy, which devastated parts of the Caribbean and the U.S. east coast in 2012, are good for economic growth. The destruction they bring is ignored, while the increase in output that comes from rebuilding adds to economic growth.

Building a prison contributes to GDP. If people burn the rain forests and plant oil palm trees, this also adds to GDP. Similarly, the removal of nuclear waste from contaminated ground adds to GDP.

So, housing more prisoners, creating ecological devastation, and cleaning up after radioactive leaks are good for economic growth.

A parent raising a child does not generate any economic growth. Teaching a child to be a good member of society, helping them develop a sense of morality, or imparting good manners are without any value, in terms of GDP. If the child is raised by a paid nanny, however, or learns to read and write at school, this adds to GDP.

From a GDP perspective, nature is worth only what can be extracted, or built upon, because everything needs to have a monetary value before it can be included. So when people build homes on flood plains or drive cargo ships through seas where there were once ice caps, GDP increases and economists and commentators are delighted because the new homes and trade generate economic growth. The value of the lost wetlands and polar ice caps is not counted.

Nor does GDP growth take any account of inequality. If there is rising wealth in an economy, but it all goes to the richest 1%, the unequal distribution is not reflected in GDP. Neither does economic growth take into account people's health or happiness. When it comes to GDP, as long as the economy grows, that is all that matters.

To highlight how unhelpful measuring GDP can be, French historian Alfred Sauvy[2] pointed out that a man who marries his cleaner reduces his nation's GDP. His wife will still clean the house, but she will no longer be paid and so will not be counted. Her work becomes economically irrelevant.

Although it may be difficult to believe, societies' focus on economic growth is a very recent phenomenon. The pace of economic growth experienced in the last thirty years is also extremely unusual. Between 1980 and 2007, the world had the fastest and the most sustained period of economic growth in more than two thousand years.

To many people, the pursuit of economic growth has become almost natural, yet for most of recorded history there was no economic growth at all. Nothing. Following the decline of the Roman Empire in around 400 CE, the economies of Europe shrank for hundreds of years.[3] Between 1000 CE and the early 1800s, they grew by only 0.3% a year,[4] practically a recession by today's standards. There was human progress during these eight hundred years, of course. The population rose, and there were many advances in technology and science. But change was almost imperceptibly slow compared to today.

For centuries, every generation lived in exactly the same way, unless there were wars or plagues, which there often were. Grandfather after grandfather would sit on the same wooden chair, at the end of the same wooden dining table, eating the same amount of the same sort of porridge with the same wooden spoon.

There was no increase in production and no economic growth.

Until the nineteenth century, it was thought that there were unbreakable laws that governed humanity. Social thinkers of the time observed that living standards stayed almost constant for centuries and believed that there was a law of nature that held the majority of people in poverty and stopped society developing any faster or getting any richer. Even when new lands were colonized or plundered, and their treasures were shipped back to Europe, the life of the average citizen did not get any better. Whenever standards of living improved just a little, the population would increase and, without any increase in food production, poverty would return. Living standards were pushed back to where they started. There seemed to be no way out of the cycle.

Observing this, Adam Smith sought to understand how it might be possible to break the pattern and improve standards of living, not just for one generation or for one part of society but in a broader and more sustainable way for the majority. This is what his famous book, written in 1776 and generally known by its short-form title, *The Wealth of Nations*,[5] is about.

People were poor, he argued, because output was too low. One way to fix this was to increase productivity, or the output per worker per year. To explain his theory, he used the example of a pin factory. Rather than having one worker produce as many pins as possible, Smith saw that productivity could be increased if the process was divided into simpler stages. If workers focused on one stage, rather than trying to do every stage themselves, the number of pins produced per worker would rise. This lowered the cost of each pin, expanding the market and allowing the business to grow. This generated more income for the owner, encouraging him to boost production and employ more people. If people had the chance to work and earn a wage, Smith reasoned, average living standards would improve.

Smith's ideas and observations were not responsible for kicking off the era of rapid economic growth, however. That began thanks to another Scot, James Watt.

For thousands of years, people had used various forms of energy to supplement human manpower. Water wheels and windmills used water and wind to increase the supply of grain. Animals attached to plows were used to raise agricultural production. Wood, charcoal, and coal made it possible to work hot metal.

By the early eighteenth century, steam engines had been developed and were being used mostly to pump water from flooded coal mines. But they were very inefficient, requiring, somewhat ironically given their primary use at the time, huge quantities of coal. After many years of working on this problem, Watt managed to increase their efficiency by adding a separate condenser and rotary motion. This dramatically lowered the production cost of coal, allowing the mine owners to sell more of it.

As with Smith's pin factory, Watt's steam engine increased productivity.

Watt's invention also made it possible for the engines to be placed anywhere there was access to water and fuel. This allowed the development of steam trains and ships, and so encouraged trade. Trade, as Smith observed, also promoted productivity growth and led to higher living standards for all.

Thanks to Watt's steam engine, Britain's weavers began to manufacture cotton more cheaply than the hand-weaving Indians. This gave birth to an entirely new industry. The mills built to spin and weave the cotton gradually changed the landscape, increasing the rate of urbanization. Other industries began to emerge, and by 1870, Britain's steam engines were generating the energy equivalent of 40 million people, allowing the country (with a population at the time of less than 30 million) to expand its output without having any more mouths to feed.

The productivity of the nation was transformed.

During the nineteenth century, steam power spread from Britain across Europe and to the United States, where it changed the agricultural industry and led to the creation of the railroads.

After many years of near stagnation, the economies of Western Europe and North America gradually took off. In Europe, the rate of economic growth rose above 2% a year after 1820, and it remained at this level for the rest of the nineteenth century.[6]

What does all this mean in economic terms? Watt's steam engine increased productivity, and so output. Energy, in the form of coal, was converted into practical forms of power (force, torque, movement, and heat), which increased the output per worker. The use of machines in factories had the same effect. The energy and mass production techniques increased productivity. They generated economic growth.

Economic growth comes mainly from rising productivity. It depends on the output per person increasing. This is important to understand, as we will come back to the issue frequently. Economic growth is not the result of rising consumption, from people buying more, despite what you might think if you read many newspaper reports. Consumption is a *consequence* of production. It is the increase in output that makes the increase in spending possible. Put simply, you can buy a bar of chocolate only if someone has first taken the trouble to make it.

Economic growth also depends on the population. If the population is rising, and if people have work and a source of income, they are able to buy things. So output will rise to meet the increase in demand. With a stable or declining population, though, as there will be in much of the developed world in the coming decades, this particular source of economic growth diminishes.

Output also increases when labor and capital are used to produce new machinery and infrastructure, and it increases when the nation produces something that other countries are willing to buy, when there is trade. We will look at this in more detail later.

What is well-being?

Well-being is difficult to define or measure accurately. It is perhaps best understood by people's answer to the question: On a scale from 0 to 10, how satisfied are you with life in general? Subjective well-being is influenced by many factors, including income. Some of the factors are more measurable than others. When people are poor (for example, when GDP per person is less than $10,000 a year—as it was in the United States in 1955 or the fifteen countries of the European Union (EU) in 1965), increasing income leads to a significant rise in self-reported ("subjective") well-being. At higher levels of income, however, the impact of higher earnings is lower, though it is still there. In rich societies, income is still important to individual well-being, but the effect is primarily relational. Middle-class people are more interested in boosting their incomes so that they keep their position in the social hierarchy and not because it allows them to buy another sofa.

Does economic growth lead to greater well-being?

It does in poor societies. Rising output tends to improve well-being when most people have low incomes. The answer is not as clear when it comes to rich nations, unfortunately. Remember, GDP measures the level of economic activity, not the level of happiness. It increases when more people work, when they create more value per person per year. But it also increases when they work on tasks that are socially undesirable, such as repairing the damage caused by climate change, work that effectively wastes human input, energy, and resources because it only fixes the unwelcome consequences of previous activities. So rising GDP does not always lead to higher average levels of well-being.

It is important to understand that economic growth is mostly dependent on improved productivity. Improved productivity means that fewer resources, in the form of workers, energy, and raw materials mostly, are required to generate a given level of output. Or, put another way, while the volume of inputs remains unchanged (workers, energy, and raw materials), the volume produced increases.

We can use Smith's pin factory as an example: Let's assume ten workers in a pin factory make one thousand pins a day. If they divide the tasks and specialize, however, they may produce ten thousand pins a day—a tenfold increase in productivity. This means the price of the pins can be reduced, making it possible to sell more pins. People get more pins per dollar, so consumption increases. The rise in productivity creates economic growth.

As long as more jobs are created, then the overall output and well-being of society tends to increase. This is what Smith believed would happen when he made his pin factory observations. But even at the time Smith was writing, and in the decades that followed, things did not turn out this way. Despite the dramatic increase in output, the effects of the first phase of the industrial revolution were awful for the vast majority. The average standard of living did not improve. In many cases it deteriorated, with millions of people worse off than before.

The cotton mills and factories were ghastly places, where children also worked, the hours were long, and the air was often so bad it was life threatening. Accidents were common and often fatal. The consequent rise in urbanization also brought slums, as well as the spread of disease and violence. Those who were unable to find work, as well as the homeless, destitute, or infirm, were typically sent to workhouses. Farmers were replaced by machines and thrown off their land. Life expectancies barely improved, and wages also remained pitifully low, because factory owners kept the profits for themselves.

There was much faster economic growth in the nineteenth century, and a progress of sorts, but almost all the benefits went to the rich. The early decades of the industrial revolution, which heralded the era of faster economic growth, did not improve the living standards of the majority.

Toward the end of the nineteenth century, the situation began to improve greatly because of the influence of the labor movement, which emerged in response to the terrible working conditions. Legislative reforms were gradually introduced to make the mills and factories safer. Thanks mostly to German engineering, the machines were made less dangerous and more efficient. Working hours fell and wages began to rise. But this particular change was not down to any benevolence on the part of the factory owners. It was because of the growing labor shortage. Faced with the choice between working in a dark satanic mill and poverty, almost a quarter of the British population emigrated, mostly to the United States, Canada, Australia, and New Zealand. Rather than live in industrial misery or destitution, they fled the country.

By the early twentieth century, the broader acceptance of workers' rights and a host of inventions gradually began to boost living standards. Cars and aircraft changed mobility. Telegraphs and telephones lowered the cost of communications. Indoor toilets, piped water, and electric light transformed people's homes. Labor shortages and the efforts of the growing trade union movement meant wages began to rise faster and eventually kicked off the virtuous cycle that the rich world enjoyed until very recently. With increasing wages there was increasing demand. This required higher output and brought higher rewards for those who paid the wages. This is one reason why Henry Ford announced in 1914 that he would pay his workers five dollars a day, far more than any of his rivals.[7] Better pay would not just make them work harder, he reasoned, it would also make them better off. Then they could buy one of his cars.

As the twentieth century progressed and standards of living rose, the slums gave way to better housing and safer streets. Healthcare improved dramatically, and infant mortality declined, increasing average life expectancies. The rich world's population increased,[8] first rapidly, then more slowly as fertility rates sank. During the twentieth century, the same demographic transition—from many children and short lives, to fewer children and longer lives—spread to the rest of the world. The well-known result was a rapid increase in the world's population, a rise that is unlikely to stop before the middle of the twenty-first century.

GRAPH I: POPULATION GROWTH WILL SLOW

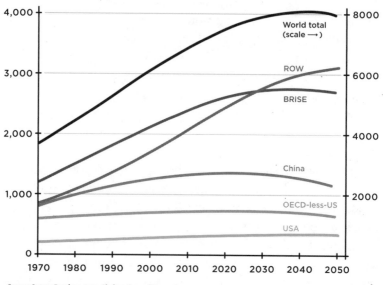

Source: Jorgen Randers, 2052, Chelsea Green, Vermont, 2012

Scale: Population in thousands of persons

The population of the world is expected to reach a peak around 2040. Most rich-world countries (OECD less the U.S.) will experience decline from now on; only the U.S. will continue to grow slowly. China is expected to remain stable at around 1.3 billion people for a decade after 2015 and then decline. Fourteen big emerging economies (BRISE) are predicted to peak in the 2030s. Only the rest of the world (ROW—140 mostly small and mostly poor nations) will continue to grow beyond 2050.

The population increase led to further economic growth.

In 1900, the United States overtook China to become the world's biggest economy. Fifty years later, the United States accounted for more than a third of global output and led the world not just economically but politically and militarily, too.[9] The effects of the relentless focus on boosting productivity, as well as openness to trade and the magic of the free market, were abundantly clear. By the last few decades of the twentieth century, they had become clearer still. The Soviet Union, with its focus on state-controlled economic growth, was close to collapse. Communist China, which had been the world's biggest economy for most of the previous thousand years and had a population five times the size of the United States, accounted for barely 3% of global output.

GRAPH 2: GDP (TOTAL OUTPUT) WILL GROW, BUT MORE SLOWLY

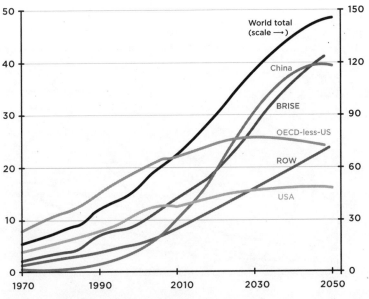

Source: Jorgen Randers, *2052*, Chelsea Green, Vermont, 2012

Scale: GDP in trillions of 2005-PPP-$ per year

The annual output of the world (its gross domestic product) is expected to grow, but ever more slowly, toward the middle of the twenty-first century and peak sometime after 2050. Most rich-world countries (OECD less the U.S.) are expected to peak around 2030 and be at 2015 levels in 2050. The U.S. will continue to grow slowly, because of immigration. China is predicted to increase its GDP by a factor of four. Fourteen big emerging economies (BRISE) will expand their GDP by a factor of three, as will the rest of the world (ROW—140 mostly small and mostly poor nations) because of rapid population growth.

In terms of GDP per person, which is a much better way to look at this transformation if you are concerned about the fate of the average citizen, the rich world leapt far ahead of every other region in the world. By 1900, the GDP per head in Western Europe, the U.S., Australia, Canada, New Zealand, and Japan[10] was four times bigger than anywhere else. By 2000, it was six times greater. For almost 100 years, the developed world accounted for more than half the world's GDP, despite never having more than a quarter of the population.[11]

GRAPH 3: GDP PER PERSON WILL GROW AT DIFFERENT SPEEDS

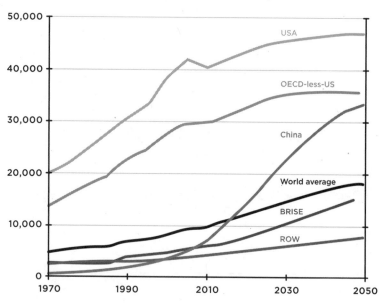

Source: Jorgen Randers, 2052, Chelsea Green, Vermont, 2012

Scale: GDP in 2005-PPP-$ per inhabitant per year

The output per person (GDP per inhabitant) will hardly grow in the rich world in the years to 2050. It is expected to explode—increase by a factor of five—in China. Half of the fourteen big emerging economies (BRISE) are predicted to follow suit; the other half will not succeed in takeoff. Growth in the rest of the world (ROW—140 mostly small and mostly poor nations) is expected to remain low toward 2050, because there will be little change in conditions for growth.

TABLE I: THE IMPACT OF RAPID ECONOMIC GROWTH, 1820 VS. 2001

	U.K.	U.K.	USA	USA
	1820	2001	1820	2001
GDP per person hour (1990$)	1.50	28.60	1.30	36.40
Average years of education per person employed	2	16	2	20
Average GDP per person (1990$)	2,075	21,565	1,360	28,725
Population (million)[12]	21	59	10	285
Hours worked per inhabitant per year[13]	1,150	700	970	770

Source: Professor Angus Maddison FBA, February 20, 2005. Evidence submitted to the Select Committee on Economic Affairs, House of Lords, London, for the inquiry into *Aspects of the Economics of Climate Change*.

Does economic growth lead to growth in GDP per person?

Not necessarily. Economic growth is the same as growth in GDP. GDP is also the GDP per person multiplied by the number of inhabitants. GDP will grow if the population grows and if the GDP per person grows. But if the population declines, GDP will decline, even if the GDP per person stays constant. Or the situation may be like Japan since 1990: stable GDP, declining population, and increasing GDP per person.

The GDP per person is the value of the annual output of goods and services in a country divided by its (average) population during the year. Measuring GDP per person helps show how well the nation has succeeded in getting its people into paid jobs. The GDP per person is higher, all other things being equal, when labor participation rates grow, when people work more hours per year, and when they work more effectively (producing more output per hour, perhaps because they are better trained or have better equipment). But higher GDP per person does not always lead to higher average well-being in the population. Above US$30,000 per person per year, it appears that many would choose shorter hours and a steady income, instead of working the same hours and having a rising income—especially if all their neighbors do the same.

Why do the people who own businesses focus on total GDP, whereas those who are employed have more interest in GDP per person?

The sales of a company tend to increase with the size of the market. The size of the market increases both with the population and with income per person. This is why businesses are interested in market growth, and the growth of total GDP, irrespective of its source. Individual workers, on the other hand, are interested in higher wages, which grow in parallel with GDP per person and are not affected by population growth.

This era of rapid economic growth brought widespread social dividends. Higher tax revenues allowed governments to build more schools. This meant that more people could be better educated and for longer.[14] Working hours gradually fell, giving people more leisure time.[15] Joblessness was low,[16] as was welfare spending. By the 1960s, most workers were even being paid while on vacation and most employers were providing pension schemes and health insurance.[17]

**GRAPH 4: THE DISPOSABLE INCOME PER PERSON WILL
REMAIN DIFFERENT AMONG THE WORLD'S REGIONS**

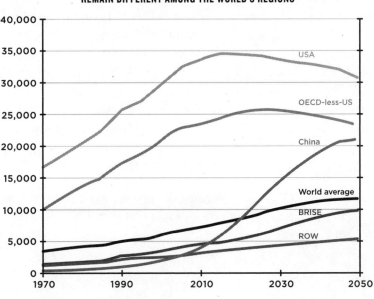

Source: Jorgen Randers, 2052, Chelsea Green, Vermont, 2012

Scale: Income in 2005-PPP-$ per inhabitant per year

The average disposable income is expected to develop similarly to the GDP per person (see Graph 3). But disposable income is expected to grow more slowly than GDP per person—and even decline—in the rich world because society will have to use ever more labor and capital to fight resource scarcity, climate change, biodiversity loss, and inequity.

The nature of work changed, too. At the beginning of the twentieth century, more than 80% of American men worked outdoors.[18] By the end of the century, 80% worked in places that were heated in winter and cooled in summer. Work was much safer, too, thanks to better production technology, unionization, and improvements in medical care.[19]

At home, machines took away much of the drudgery of housework, freeing the average housewife from more than twenty hours of domestic work a week.[20] The availability of running water, electricity, and constant light, as well as modern appliances such as washing machines, irons, and refrigerators, significantly reduced the time demands on women in the home. This allowed the number of women in the workplace to rise dramatically, offering them greater independence.[21]

Life expectancies gradually increased. With the drop in infant mortality, improved nutrition, and better healthcare, people born in the rich world at the end of the twentieth century were expected to live almost fifty years longer than those born one hundred years before.

TABLE 2: POPULATION, MILLION PEOPLE

	1900	1950	2001
W Europe	234	305	392
United States	76	125	285
Other*	10	24	55
Japan	44	84	127
Total "West"	364	565	859
World	1,564	2,524	6,149

Source: Maddison, *Aspects of the Economics of Climate Change*, 2005, p. 5, Table 2.
Other* = refers to Australia, Canada, and New Zealand

As wages rose and poverty declined, the gap between rich and poor narrowed, though this was not just thanks to economic development. It was also because of the increase in output necessitated by two colossal industrialized wars and the state intervention this required.

In 1917, the United States' richest 5% took home 33% of the total income generated by the economy.[22] By 1953, their share had dropped to 20%, and the share taken by the top 1% had almost halved, to 28%.[23] In Canada, Germany, France, Italy, and much of the rest of Europe, inequality fell even faster. In the Netherlands,

Denmark, Finland, and Norway, the gap narrowed more dramatically still.

This change is especially important because if the gap between rich and poor is narrow, people are generally happier and healthier. Measuring inequality is a good supplement to GDP per person if you want to track social well-being. When inequality is low, countries tend to be more stable, more tolerant, and more law abiding, with fewer people in prison or sleeping on the streets. People live longer, too.[24]

Does economic growth always bring more jobs?

Economic growth usually brings more jobs. The number of jobs in an economy increases when GDP grows faster than average labor productivity. But since labor productivity is normally measured as output per hour, and GDP as output per year, society can also increase the number of full-time jobs simply by reducing the length of the work year (the number of hours worked per year per person in a full-time job). Of course, rising GDP does not always mean that jobs will be created. For example, GDP also grows when many small labor-
intensive businesses are replaced by one capital-intensive factory with few operators.

Does economic growth always reduce inequality?

It depends on how the resulting output is distributed. If the value added is split evenly among all citizens, economic growth leads to greater equality. If one group, say the wealthy, takes more than their fair share, growth increases inequality. Redistribution of income (which is generally understood to mean taking from the rich and giving to the poor) is difficult and normally only achieved through strong labor unions and government intervention.

A simple measure of equality is the workers' share of the national income (the "wage share"). The wage share increased after World War II in most rich countries, meaning there was greater equality, but fell back again after 1990 in many rich countries, especially the U.S. Another simple indicator of equality is the Palma ratio, which shows the percentage of national income going to the richest 10% of the population divided by the share of income received by the poorest 40%. In 2015, the Palma ratio was around 2 in the U.S. and around 1 in more egalitarian Scandinavia.

By the 1950s, the benefits of economic growth, once the total income had been more evenly spread across the population, had become truly remarkable. There was a vast improvement in standards of living, much lower unemployment, increased leisure time, reduced inequality, and higher life expectancies. Economic growth boosted education standards and made people happier. For decades, the pursuit of economic growth achieved all that people like to think it still does, and more.

It achieved much more. The fact that most people in the developed world have the right to vote today is greatly thanks to the era of rapid economic development. The terrible conditions workers had to endure in the nineteenth century, at the start of the industrial age, led them to demand change. Once they had achieved that, it was a small step for them to demand a say in how the world was run. It was the opportunity to increase output that led to the factory. It was the factory that led to the exploitation of workers. It was the exploitation that forced the workers to fight for their rights. And it was this fight that led to greater democratic rights for everyone.

The fact that the United States' minorities, and most of the rich world's women, have much greater equality today is also greatly down to this era of economic growth. The years of growth freed the underprivileged from their chains, by offering them work and other opportunities, and by changing the way people think about equality.

In the United States and some other parts of the rich world today, certain groups seek to deny how these social changes came about. Employees are put under enormous pressure to reject being part of any organized group that challenges the will of business owners today. Yet much of the success of the United States' remarkable development does not rest with those who established the factories and wanted to keep all the rewards for themselves. It rests with the workers who demanded better working conditions and found the courage to fight for their rights. This is where the foundations of the United States' freedoms lie.

Today's U.S. working class has been talked into believing that unionization is no longer necessary, and the middle classes think that it is not in their interests. As we will discuss in the next chapter, this lies at the heart of many of the changes that American workers have experienced since the early 1980s—falling wages, longer hours, and fewer benefits.

The rapid pace of economic development during the twentieth century in the rich world is also the reason why its physical infrastructure is generally better than elsewhere, though this is no longer the case in the United States. During the boom years, as the working population earned more, taxes allowed Western governments to spend more. This allowed them to construct bigger and better hospitals, roads, ports, and tunnels, which extended their advantage over their developing world rivals.

Bigger economies also gave the West more political clout. They offered the high-income world a stage from which to encourage others to follow its way of thinking. After all, why would the developing world not want something that offered so many advantages? Greater economic scale made it easier for the United States to demand less regulation and more open markets in other parts of the world. It allowed the United States and the rest of the developed world to nudge other countries onto the same economic path—often at a faster pace. There is only one way to develop, the developing world was told, and this is it. The era of rapid economic growth gave the rich world the chance to create new markets in its own image, to the benefit of its own citizens and businesses.

For decades, economic growth was the magic dust that transformed almost everything it touched.

As we will show in the next chapter, though, that magic dust has stopped working.

CHAPTER 3

THE OLD APPROACH
NO LONGER WORKS

*For many years the pursuit of economic growth has not
reduced unemployment. It has increased inequality.*

"Capitalism is the extraordinary belief that the nastiest of men, for
the nastiest of motives, will somehow work for the benefit of all."
JOHN MAYNARD KEYNES

I N 1930, ECONOMIST John Maynard Keynes predicted that his
grandchildren would need to work only fifteen hours a week.[1] By
the time they were of working age, he reasoned, there would be
sufficient economic output and the citizens of the rich world would
be able to spend their lives working less and doing more of what they
wanted. The rich world could focus on leisure, science, and the pursuit of greater knowledge, he thought.

Keynes's prediction could certainly have been fulfilled by the
end of the twentieth century. The average GDP per person in the
rich world—at more than US$35,000[2]—was enough for everyone to
live reasonably comfortably. The surge in social progress and output
Keynes had anticipated in the 1930s had happened pretty much as
he predicted, yet unemployment was high throughout the Organisa-
tion for Economic Co-operation and Development (OECD) nations,
working hours were often longer than in the 1930s, and inequalities
had widened.

The problem was that the income, work, and wealth that had
been created were very unevenly divided. By the early years of the
twenty-first century, a small percentage of the population had

become very rich, while tens of millions still lived in poverty—some of it extreme. The 2008 financial crisis widened the gap between rich and poor even further.[3]

How did this happen? If economic growth improves average living standards and spreads the wealth more evenly, as economists say, why was the gap between rich and poor so wide—and getting wider? Was it simply a short-term problem, the result of the dot-com bubble bursting in 2000 and the 2008 financial crisis, for example? Or was something else going on?

GRAPH 5: INEQUALITY IS INCREASING, ESPECIALLY IN THE U.S.

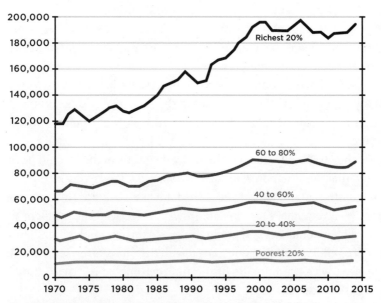

Source: U.S. Census Bureau, Current Population Survey, Annual Social and Economic Supplements.
https://www.census.gov/hhes/www/income/data/historical/inequality/

Scale: Income in 2014-$ per household per year

The annual income of the richest 20% of U.S. households doubled from 1970 to 2014 (top black curve). The income of the 40% poorest households did not change at all—it has remained constant in real terms for more than forty-five years. The middle-class households (those ranking between 40% and 80% on an income scale) increased their incomes by approximately one third over the same forty-five years. Only the rich got significantly richer.

In 2008, many economists claimed that the financial crisis was an unexpected and temporary problem, a mere hiccup in an otherwise reliable system. They said that the problem could be fixed if governments stimulated more economic growth. With greater growth, unemployment would fall and average standards of living would start to recover. Thanks to the trickle-down effect, the gap between rich and poor would soon narrow again.

At the time, we read this advice with a skeptical eye. We did not think these economists were correct. More economic growth would not solve the problems of unemployment and widening inequality, we said. Rather, we argued, it would make the problems worse.

Most people seemed to think we were slightly mad.

We saw that mainstream economists, bankers, and growth-hungry businesspeople had not understood that the economic environment had fundamentally changed. They had simply looked to the past, seen that economic growth had been remarkably successful for many years and, without examining the reasons for this, assumed that the pursuit of more growth was still the right policy for the future.

If they had scratched a little below the surface, they would have found that the situation was not as it appeared. Real living standards for hundreds of millions of people had not been rising for many years, despite strong headline rates of growth. Moreover, the problem of widening inequalities and gradually increasing unemployment (and underemployment) had not started with the financial crisis in 2008, nor even with the bursting of the Internet bubble in 2000. It had started decades before.

A deeper analysis revealed that economic growth had increased the average purchasing power of Western citizens only up to the early 1980s. After that, declines in the price of many goods led to continued reductions in the cost of clothes, cars, and groceries, and this had made people continue to feel better off. Easier borrowing had led to steadily rising house prices, which had made people think they were rich. There were all sorts of stunning technological developments, too, from the invention of the Internet to the introduction of life-changing gadgets such as cell phones and home computers. These had made the majority of people feel as though they were still living in an era of incredible and rapid social progress. And to all appearances, they were.

But real wages in parts of the developed world had actually been falling. By 2014, more than half the U.S. working population was earning less, in real terms, than it had in 1979. The U.S. economy had grown by more than 140%, but the poorest 20% of the population had seen its income fall, whereas the richest 20% had seen its income more than double.

Since as far back as the early 1960s, the minimum wage in the United States had been falling in real terms while the proportion of workers earning it had risen.[4] In other words, an increasing number of people had been earning a lower real wage. Other employment benefits had also been cut. Significantly fewer companies contributed to the pensions of their employees in 2014 than in the 1980s, for example, and most of those that did still contribute no longer made any promises about what sort of pension their workers might receive. Company-funded health insurance had been taken away from huge numbers of employees, too.[5] Union memberships had also sharply declined,[6] strengthening the power of business owners.

Despite falling wages, working hours had risen. In 1975, the average U.S. worker (including those working part time) put in 1,705 hours a year. A generation later, in 2011, they worked 1,863 hours— 9% more.[7]

Keynes would have found all this very difficult to understand. With so much economic and material progress, how could the working year have increased like this, particularly when productivity had been rising steadily? In 1979, the value of the output of every U.S. citizen stood at just under $25,000 a year (see Graph 3). By 2011, it had risen to $40,000—even in real terms. Yet wages had fallen and working hours had increased. This meant that businesses had been making people work harder, so increasing efficiency, while simultaneously lowering wages to boost profits.

Why were they doing that?

The short answer is that businesses were cutting wages and boosting profits because that is what the free-market economic system increasingly demanded. Stock markets and the finance sector had become more influential, and those who worked in those sectors, as well as company stockholders, expected ever-higher quarterly returns. There was enormous pressure from "the market," in other words, for businesses to eke out the best returns, to shift their head offices offshore, to cut employee costs, to move factories to low-cost countries, to collaborate to reduce the costs of raw materials, and to demand less red tape, tax, and regulation. Without any strong counterbalancing force—from society, the unions, or employees—businesses were passing fewer and fewer of their gains onto their staff or society.

On the surface then, there was progress. Economies were growing and businesses were doing nicely. Profits and productivity were rising, and stock markets were booming. Low interest rates and easy credit meant house prices were higher, too. Between 1980 and 2010, the U.S. economy expanded at an average rate of 2.9% a year,[8] a remarkable clip for such an economically mature country, and it was much the same in the rest of the OECD countries.

It looked, at least superficially, as if the pursuit of economic growth was still having its magical effect. This is why most economists and politicians would continue to claim that economic growth, and Gordon Gekko's infamous greed, was still good. It did not matter to them that the underlying social trends showed something completely different. For those on Wall Street and the rich, the boom years and the pursuit of growth were still great.

In reality, the rising incomes of the rich and changes to the tax system were widening the gap between rich and poor all the time. In 1960, the richest 0.1% in the United States paid an average effective federal tax rate of 71%. Forty-five years later, this had plummeted to just under 35%, whereas the average tax rate for 80% of the population had gone up.[9]

Although the economy had been booming, poverty in much of the rich world had been rising. This was not what free-market ideologues had predicted (or even claimed was happening). Rather than spreading the wealth around, the boom had allowed a small percentage of the population to hoard a disproportionately large share of the gains, while the living standards of millions of people throughout the developed world moved in the opposite direction.

The legacy of more than thirty years of rapid economic development is almost 50 million Americans living in poverty, with 44% of them in "deep poverty," meaning their incomes are less than half the government-defined poverty level.[10] One in every six households and one in every four people under the age of eighteen in the United States are now below the official poverty line.[11]

In the rest of the rich world, the picture is much the same. Real wages in the U.K. have been falling since 2003, and working hours have increased.[12] A growing number of people in Britain also now work under employment contracts that do not even guarantee them a certain number of working hours per week, so-called zero-hours contracts.

Unemployment has risen throughout the rich world. Between 1980 and 2014, joblessness throughout the OECD averaged more than 7%, far higher than it had been in the 1950s and 1960s.[13] In the European Union, it is still above 9% in 2016, with minorities and the young particularly badly affected.[14] In 2000, almost 30%[15] of U.S. college graduates under twenty-four were under-employed.[16] Ten years later, 40% were jobless, with many also heavily in debt because of student loans. In much of southern Europe—Spain and Greece, in particular—youth unemployment remained above 50% in 2016.

The length of unemployment periods has also changed. After World War II, people were typically jobless for a few weeks or months at a time, even when there were rising numbers of immigrants enlarging the job pool. In the late 1960s, fewer than 5% of those registered as unemployed in the United States had been without work for twenty-seven months or more. Today, 44% of those without jobs have not had work for more than two years.

This raises an important question.

With so many people out of work and lower average real incomes, how did the rich-world economies manage to keep growing? The GDP of the richest countries was more than twice as big in 2010 as it was in 1980[17] (see Graph 2), but apart from a few brief periods, there has been continuous growth. How was it possible for these economies to continue to expand so quickly when fewer people had jobs and average incomes were stagnant or falling?

The answer to this question is debt. For years, people in the rich world had borrowed to consume, to keep the economic growth juggernaut on the road.

At the end of World War II, the total debts (credit card, housing loans, etc.) of the average American could be paid off with around three months' take-home pay.[18] By 1980, this had risen to eight and a half months. At the peak of the financial crisis, just over twenty-five years later, it was sixteen months—133% of an annual income. It has barely changed since, leaving millions trapped with such high debts that it is almost impossible for them to borrow more. And since debt requires regular interest payments and usually some element of capital repayment, people cannot pay off their debts without reducing their spending and negatively affecting their well-being. Declaring bankruptcy might help temporarily, but it also hampers their ability to borrow—and so spend—in the future.

It was borrowing that greatly fueled the United States' economic growth until the financial crisis. And it was much the same in most of Europe, as well as in Australia and Canada. Rising debt made it possible for people to maintain their spending.

Unfortunately, borrowing as a source of demand growth is now mostly over, and spending has fallen back to something nearer the level that people on low incomes can afford once they have made the minimum payments on their credit cards and other debts each month. This is one of the main reasons why the rate of economic growth has remained low in recent years.

Is it possible to create economic growth by allowing people to borrow more?

Yes, but only for a limited time. Debt-financed consumption can only last until the consumer has borrowed so much that the lender no longer dares to lend them any more. As long as the debt is rising, the consumer can maintain a higher rate of spending than before they started their borrowing spree. But when they are unable to borrow more, spending is forced down—and to a lower level than before the borrowing began. The difference— that is, the reduction—equals the amount the borrower has to pay in interest and in repayment of the loan. Borrowing simply makes it possible to increase consumption above what is sustainable for a limited period of time. It cannot lift the rate of consumption in the long term.

We can look at the debt phenomenon another way. The increase in debt meant that the poor (and their consumption) were funded by the rich, whose savings were loaned through the banking system. In effect, the rich boosted their incomes by paying the poor less than before (and making them work longer hours into the bargain). They then became richer still by lending the poor the profits, in return for interest. So it is not just rising business profits and lower taxes that have benefited the wealthiest segments of society. Nor is it purely falling wages and rising unemployment that have blighted the poor. The great borrowing binge of the last three decades has also greatly widened the gap between rich and poor by increasing the flow of money to the rich.

The combined effect of these trends is startling. Instead of three decades of economic growth improving average living standards, as economists said it would, it has led to a decline in living standards for vast numbers of people. Rather than creating jobs and narrowing the gap between rich and poor as expected, millions of people in the rich world are being thrown back to a place they have not occupied for almost a century. In the United States, the U.K., and Ireland, the gap between rich and poor is bigger today than it was in 1917, a remarkable reversal of economic and social progress.[19]

It is not the same everywhere, however. The gap between rich and poor in Japan has not widened much. Nor has inequality changed much in Germany, Sweden, or much of the rest of Europe in the last thirty years, despite the hike in unemployment. Inequality has actually fallen slightly in France, Norway, and Italy, as well as in Canada, though it has risen there again since 2011. This is because the unemployed are better supported and the wealthy more highly taxed in these countries.[20]

This at least shows that it is possible to live in the developed world, to run an open free-market economy, to have experienced thirty years of spectacular economic growth, to have a financial crisis, to have unemployment rise, and still see no widening of inequalities.

It is possible if the extreme effects of the free-market model are properly managed.

In many other OECD countries, though, and most notably in the places inhabited by the loudest proponents of the extreme free-market ideology, the economic growth of the last thirty years has not distributed incomes and wealth more evenly. It has not created enough jobs. It has achieved the opposite.[21]

DESPITE ALL THIS, most rich-world economists and politicians still think that pushing for faster economic growth is a good idea. They still believe that free-market economic thinking can reduce unemployment and inequality. Like captains of a ship that has veered wildly off course and then hit a rock, they think the solution is to push the engines harder rather than to properly understand what is going on. Few have questioned the fundamental wisdom of having a lightly regulated free-market economic system, even though it has not done what it promised for so long.

Rather than trying to bring their economies into balance, rich-world governments have continued as before. As a consequence, the developed world's economy is becoming more and more like one of those cartoon characters that has run off a cliff, legs still running furiously, despite there being no solid ground beneath them. It is riddled with financial imbalances and burdened with trillions of dollars in debts that are unlikely to ever be repaid. The entire system is off course.

Since 2008, in addition to implementing their usual economic strategies, rich-world governments have employed two especially important and unusual policies to respond to the current challenges: ultra-low interest rates and Quantitative Easing (QE),[22] which just means printing money. Governments and businesses have also applied enormous psychological pressure on their citizens to continue spending, encouraging them to borrow more if necessary, to maintain economic growth. Many banks have received cash injections to strengthen their balance sheets and access to low-cost central bank funding to maintain liquidity and boost lending.

As a result, commercial rates of interest in much of the rich world are at their lowest level ever,[23] with several European countries, the eurozone, and Japan offering negative rates, forcing people to pay to save (thereby encouraging them to spend instead).

The consequences of lowering the costs of borrowing like this are that bankers and the rich have gained even more. Between 2008 and 2013, commercial banks increased their profits because their margins (the difference between the rate at which they borrow and lend) rose. Many big corporations also gained, through lower interest payments, while financial investors, such as venture capitalists and hedge funds, were able to borrow more cheaply, allowing them to snap up assets before they increased in value.

Developed-world households were the main losers from the low interest rate policy, suffering $630 billion in lost interest income between 2007 and the end of 2013.[24] Those living off their bank savings were hit especially hard. European banks and life insurance companies also lost out, because of the decline in interest income. Many pension funds had problems, too. As their earnings declined, some found themselves unable to meet their future commitments.

As with the wider free-market economic system, the main beneficiaries of this low interest rate policy were the wealthy, especially
in the United States, and the finance industry. In effect, ultra-low
interest rates increased the flow of money from those who borrow
(generally, the poor) to those who lend (generally, the rich), widening
inequality even more.

It is much the same with QE.

After the 2008 financial crisis, there was a risk of deflation, when
average prices fall. For economists, this is a scary prospect because
deflation is extremely hard to cure. When prices fall, people delay
spending because they know that whatever they want to buy will be
cheaper in the future. Deflation causes the economy to slow and then
shrink, with nasty implications for jobs, wages, and asset values.

To avoid this risk, economists advised governments to print
money, which is thought to have an inflationary effect.

Between 2008 and October 2014, the United States' central bank,
the Federal Reserve, injected between $75 billion and $85 billion into
the economy every month. Cumulatively, it injected $4.5 trillion—
more than a quarter of the country's annual GDP. This was the same
as adding another Australia, India, and Spain to the world economy.

The British government did much the same, injecting $500 bil-
lion, while the Bank of Japan and the European Central Bank (ECB)
also printed many hundreds of billions of yen and euros—and continue to print them today, in 2016.

Together, these countries have injected so much money into the
global economies since 2008 that it has been like adding another
China.[25] If this money was simply converted to demand and output,
it would have increased the GDP of these countries by more than
25% between 2008 and 2015. Yet their GDP grew by just 11% in real
terms. The rest was kept by business owners and banks, or used to
boost asset prices.

Essentially, all this money was created out of thin air, by changing numbers on balance sheets. So, even to describe it as "printing
money" is a misnomer—no real effort was required, and certainly no
printing presses were involved. It was fed into the economy mostly
by central banks purchasing government and corporate bonds,

which were typically sold by private banks and other financial institutions, including insurance companies and pension funds. The process provided liquidity, and so cash flow, for these institutions and an opportunity for them to reinvest. The money did not go to the people—and certainly not to all those unemployed who lacked an income, which would have been much more effective. If they had been given the money, they would have spent it immediately—and created the demand that the economy needed.

As with ultra-low interest rates, the main beneficiaries of QE were business owners and financial institutions, who used the increased cash flow to boost their earnings. Or to put it another way, money was created out of thin air by central bankers and paid to bondholders, which allowed them to get richer.

Why does it not work to print money and give it to the rich?

When a central bank prints money under traditional Quantitative Easing (QE), the money is put into circulation by the bank buying bonds from bondholders. The central bank holds the bonds (and the associated interest income), and the former bondholder (typically a person who is rich enough to save and to keep part of their wealth in the form of bonds) ends up with more cash in the bank.

The former bondholder then looks for investment opportunities, for ways to get a higher return on their money. If there is unmet demand in the economy, they may choose to invest in new productive capacity—in new factories or retail stores, for example—which is what governments hope will happen. But if there is no unmet demand, but lots of overcapacity, as existed after 2008 in the rich world, they will typically look for another store of value: real estate, stocks and shares, art, metals, and so on—none of which create many new jobs.

In this situation, the more money a government prints, the more demand there is for assets. The price of those assets then increases endlessly, as the amount of cash in circulation rises.

The result is asset inflation—well known from the post-2008 period—with booming stock markets, art markets, and property values.

That this process continued—that the money was not given to the poor instead, to stimulate demand—illustrates the strong influence of the wealthy (and free-market thinking) on current economic policy.

Since the early 1980s, then, many of the cherished assumptions that underpin free-market economics have been wrong. The belief that economic growth is always good is no longer true, unless you are rich. Economic growth in the rich world has not improved living standards for the majority. It has not created jobs, or at least it has not created enough of them. And it has not reduced inequality.

Printing money and ultra-low interest rates have not achieved what they promised either. They have not led to an economic rebound, full employment, or reduced inequality.

Before we look at how societies can actually fix these problems, there is another issue that needs to be addressed.

Over the next twenty years, unless there is a change in direction, unemployment is going to rise sharply in the rich world because of new technology. Increased computerization will boost business profits, improve productivity, and create lots of new opportunities for entrepreneurs. It will also bring economic growth. But it will increase joblessness and widen the gap between rich and poor further still.

This challenge is the subject of our next chapter.

CHAPTER 4

RANDERMAXTONBOT
YOUR KIDS,
AND HOW
TO NOT
KILL
THEM

A BOOK ON SAVING
HUMANKIND ... NICELY

NEW BOOK BY
FAMOUS AUTHORBOT
RANDERMAXTONBOT

ADVANCING ROBOTIZATION

Without change, the problems of unemployment and inequality
will worsen in the next twenty years. There will also be an
unstoppable decline in the rate of conventional economic growth and
a wave of robotization in manufacturing and repetitive services.

This new medical app on my phone is amazing! It synchs with the RFID
tag in my jacket and all of my telemetry data is uploaded to a centralized
database that auto-adjusts my meds mix to control my glucose. Need an
adjustment? The drone from Walmart delivers what I need to my drone-
dock overnight—anywhere in the world! It is amazing…! On the other
hand, I want to sell my house—why isn't anyone bidding on it? There used
to be a lot of doctors in this neighborhood didn't there? Also, there used
to be a ton of delivery-drivers who came into my restaurant for breakfast
every morning… wonder where they are…? If I don't start to generate
some revenue soon, how am I going to pay my mortgage until I find a
buyer? Maybe I should get one of those robot cooks that I keep hearing
about to lower my operating costs…[1]

THE SUBSTITUTION OF humans by machines is something economists call "technological unemployment," and it is as old as humankind itself. Even the caveman's humble wheel made people redundant, because one person with a cart was able to push the same weight that several people had previously carried on their backs.

Today, the technologies used to replace people are rather different. It is now robots, computers, and other high-tech gadgets that are making people redundant, not wheels or sharpened flints.

At the beginning of the economic development process, as more capital is added, the agricultural sector gradually becomes more mechanized, and fewer people are needed to feed the population, so they move into manufacturing, the secondary economic sector. Then, as the manufacturing factories are equipped with machines, energy, and computers, fewer workers are needed there, so people focus on the next level of demand in society: services—the tertiary sector. Yet again, technological advances—this time in the form of computerization and robotization—gradually reduce the need for labor in repetitive service jobs. This frees people to do what machines cannot easily do—provide care, culture, and creativity. This is the fourth, and now emerging, economic sector.

Thanks to all sorts of remarkable developments in computing and robotics, many commentators and analysts believe that society is in the early stages of a new industrial revolution, one with the capacity to transform the way people live and work, just as the steam engine did two hundred years ago.

Computerization has already given lots of people the chance to develop exciting new careers and found new businesses. These new technologies could further transform societies and offer everyone the chance of more leisure time—depending, of course, on how they are introduced and how the rewards are divided.

The worry is what the new technologies could mean for jobs.

Technological unemployment is one of the main reasons joblessness has risen throughout the OECD during the last thirty years.[2] Although some of this is down to demographics and the changing economic structure of the rich world, the development of computers, as well as other sorts of automation and the Internet, has played a very large part, particularly since 2000. This explains why productivity in the United States rose by 2.5% a year in the first decade of the twenty-first century, while the number of available jobs fell by more than 1% a year.[3]

With the anticipated growth in computing power, the rate of technological unemployment is expected to rise in the coming decades, and most people are unprepared for what this might mean. As *The Economist* magazine put it, "the effect of today's technology on tomorrow's jobs will be immense—and no country is ready."[4]

A well-known, though perhaps slightly alarmist, study published in 2014 by Oxford University's Martin School[5] suggested that as many as 47% of all U.S. jobs are at risk in the next two decades of being mechanized or partly mechanized and so largely eradicated by the next generation of smart machines. In economic terms, this means that fewer people will be needed to produce the same output. Costs will be lower and average earnings, for those left with a job, could be higher. But there will be fewer people with jobs.

The vulnerable jobs are not only those of factory machinists, retail workers, airport check-in staff, and burger flippers. Those employed doing packaging, logistics, and deliveries are at risk of redundancy, too. Thanks to clever computer algorithms, much of the work currently done by lawyers and bankers is also threatened. The research that armies of junior financiers do could be automated as well, with big data taking on the role of today's market and business sector analysts.

Computers will even be able to replace many in the medical profession. Machines can already diagnose many diseases better than doctors and track the progress of many treatments more effectively, and image processors can analyze biopsies more accurately than lab technicians.

Thanks greatly to work done by Google, it may be possible to replace many bus, taxi, and van drivers, too (once the issue of liability insurance has been resolved). Train drivers and pilots can also be replaced, as can many university lecturers. Students may not like learning everything online, and bus passengers might feel uneasy about not having a driver, but they may have little option, because it will be cheaper.

According to the Oxford study, there is a risk, too, that much of the accountancy profession could disappear. Even journalists and soldiers are threatened with having to find new careers. Computers can already write articles well enough to replace sports and financial writers, and soldiers are being supplanted on the battlefield by robots and remotely controlled drones. The jobs of many hotel receptionists, cooks, and porters are said to be at risk, too.

Many export jobs in China and other countries with low labor costs could also disappear. If it is cheaper to manufacture goods with robots, many of the factories that moved to China and elsewhere in the last twenty-five years could move back to the developed world to reduce transport costs, though they will not bring many jobs.

Most jobs will remain, of course. The work of actors and actresses will be extremely hard to mechanize, though not impossible. A lot can be done using computer animation these days, as many photographic models may soon discover to their cost. Societies will still need to have firefighters, as well as clergy. Other reasonably secure jobs include care workers, dentists, and (some) fruit pickers. Those who offer warm hands in hospitals and nursing homes cannot easily be replaced either (though the Japanese are trying[6]). Strategic planners and barristers will always be in high demand, as well as athletes, artisans, florists, and hairdressers. Composers, novelists, and speakers' agents will not be short of work in the future much either.

At the end of its report, the Oxford study contains a list of 702 jobs, ranked according to the likelihood of their being eradicated over the next two decades. It makes for interesting reading. If you want to ask yourself how safe your own job is, then the words you need to consider are: personal care, creativity, dexterity, perception, social intelligence, and originality. If your job needs these, you are pretty safe.

The jobs that are least vulnerable are those that require high levels of education or considerable skill—which will be very well paid—as well as those that generally require dexterity, repetitiveness, creativity, or physical presence—which will not be very well paid.

Even if a fraction of these anticipated changes occurred, there would be a revolution in the workplace—with widespread social consequences. Unless the transition is managed carefully, society could become even more polarized, with a small elite gaining the chance to earn even more, while the majority earns even less.

Moreover, the jobs that remain would be bitterly fought over because, in simple economic terms, the supply of workers will greatly exceed the demand, so the price of the average employee will fall. Social mobility would be reduced, too, because the options available to job seekers will shrink.

With fewer people working, less tax would be paid into government coffers. With higher unemployment, demand for welfare would rise.

There is, therefore, a risk that this wave of robotization and mechanization might overwhelm rich-world societies, cutting average wages more, widening social divisions further, and inflaming political discord as too many people chase too few jobs. As David Ricardo, a nineteenth-century economist who studied the effects of new technology on wages during the industrial revolution, showed, there is a risk that many people's wages could fall below the level necessary for them to live.

Ricardo, who was greatly influenced by his close contemporary Adam Smith, realized that although new technologies increase business profits, they do not always increase workers' incomes. He pointed out that, in general, new technologies tend to make life better for everyone, partly because they increase productivity and cut costs. They increase output. They also encourage innovation and retraining, as those who are forced out of work need to develop new skills to become competitive in the job market again.

But he also saw that there is a short-term price to pay for new technological development: higher unemployment and lower wages. These are generally outweighed by the long-term advantages—higher productivity, lower costs, more output, greater innovation, and self-improvement—but not always.

If the long-term benefits accrue mostly to businesses, if they only increase profits and not total wages, then the new technology does not benefit the majority. As Ricardo noted, "[New technology] may increase the net revenue of the country, [but] may at the same time render the population redundant." He went on to say that the impression often held by workers and trade unionists that new technology was against their interests was "not founded on prejudice or error."[7] It was quite correct.

Although he was writing in the early nineteenth century, his observations are still valid. There is a risk that today's new computer and robot technologies could transform rich-world economies and people's lifestyles in many beneficial ways but also increase long-term joblessness and inequality.

In their two books on the subject of machines creating technological unemployment, Erik Brynjolfsson and Andrew McAfee[8] at MIT see the changes as positive. "There has never been a better time to be a talented entrepreneur," they say.[9]

We are less sure. It may well be that this is a great time "to be a talented entrepreneur," but it is also a very bad time to be a worker with a repetitive job. Human ingenuity may certainly create many new types of work, but it would take an awful lot of creativity to replace in a short time the tens of millions of jobs that are at risk in the meantime. Besides, not everyone wants to run their own business—most people just want someone to give them a job and pay them regularly. So we think it unlikely the counter-wave of entrepreneurial activity will happen fast enough or on a large enough scale to compensate for the likely rise in unemployment.

Moreover, for many people, the question will be: Retrain and do what? During the industrial revolution, it was relatively easy to take those who had toiled in the fields and provide them with a basic education. It is harder to see how society can make a step change of this sort now.

Societies have always had to adapt to new technologies, of course, and the transition is often more difficult and unpredictable than the effect of the new technologies themselves. When steam engines increased productivity in Britain in the nineteenth century and millions were left without work, they emigrated to countries where their prospects were better. Much the same happened in Russia, Italy, Scandinavia, and Germany, to name only a few. That will not be an option this time, as the introduction of these technologies will be global.

What is labor productivity, and how does it compare to GDP per person?

Labor productivity is the dollar value of the goods and services produced by a worker in a unit of time, typically an hour. Unfortunately, it does not move in parallel with output per worker per year of employment, because the number of hours worked in a year may change—for example, when the number of vacation days increases, or when people move from full-time to part-time jobs. The debate is further confused by the fact that labor productivity (output per worker-hour) is not the same as GDP per person (output per inhabitant-year). The latter spreads the total output over all citizens, not only the working population, and changes when labor participation rates change. But all three are measures of the value of economic output divided by people and time.

What is the economic impact of more robotization?

Robotization makes it possible for fewer workers to produce the same output as before, while the resulting superfluous workers are set free to do something else. It increases the labor productivity of those who still have a job and leads to higher output from each of them. Robotization makes it possible for businesses to pay higher wages or boost their profits.

In theory, and in a "perfect market," where there is lots of competition, everyone has equal access to the same information, barriers to entry and exit are low, and everyone has equal access to labor, land, capital, and energy, the extra income that new technologies generate is quickly converted into "new" demand. This creates jobs in "new" production—enough to absorb the workers who were "set free." In a perfect market, the long-term impact of robotization is to increase both output and income per worker, leading to higher GDP per person.

Ideally then, robotization (and the introduction of any new productivity-enhancing technology) should take place in a perfect market under conditions of full employment so that the benefits are fairly distributed among workers and business owners.

Unfortunately, the current economic world is far from perfect and the approaching wave of robotization is likely to come so quickly that the transition will be fraught with difficulties. The main problem is that the people who own the businesses are likely to take most of the benefits for themselves. So the profits of robot- ized companies will rise, while wage levels are kept low, or even fall, because of the abundance of labor in the economy. Since business owners today do not tend to invest their extra profits but instead save them, the "new" demand for investment goods and services will not arise quickly enough to absorb the superfluous workers.

In macroeconomic terms, the short-term effects of the coming wave of robotization will have little effect on total GDP. The same output will simply be made by fewer hands. But there will be more unemployment and greater inequality. Robotization will have no effect on the average GDP per person, but there will be fewer jobs because of the higher productivity of those who work.

Robotization also increases business profits—unless the gains are taxed.

Changing this is difficult, because it is hard to identify exactly which profits and extra wages arise directly from robotization. Society could, of course, tax robots or ban their rapid introduction. Governments could even insist on state ownership of robots to ensure that the resulting profits are distributed fairly. But all such proposals would be met by strong opposition in most rich nations and so have no chance of being accepted. As we will explain later, the only solution we see to this problem is to provide higher unemployment benefits and a guaranteed livable income, for those who need it, financed through higher taxes. In this way, the political majority could ensure that enough of the proceeds of robotization are made available for consumers to maintain demand and create the economic foundation for new jobs.

The anticipated increase in computerization, robotization, and mechanization will accelerate another trend, one that is barely discussed today but is hugely important: the potential for long-term productivity growth.

To economists, labor productivity refers to the change in the produced output per worker-hour of input. In Adam Smith's pin factory, which we discussed in Chapter 2, labor productivity rose because the factory was reorganized so that workers could specialize. Rather than every worker performing a series of identical tasks, they each performed just one task repetitively. This increased the total output of the factory without increasing the number of workers. The output per worker rose—both per hour and per year—and there was economic growth.

As with GDP growth, productivity growth is a crude measure. It says nothing about the *quality* of what is happening. If people build polluting coal-fired power stations more quickly using the same number of workers, for example, it will increase labor productivity. But it will also ruin the environment. Similarly, a musician could play a Beethoven symphony faster than intended, or a doctor could treat patients more quickly than is good for their health. A barber could cut hair faster. At a certain point, though, boosting labor productivity like this is simply undesirable or physically impossible.

To us, there are good productivity improvements and there are bad productivity improvements, just like there is good economic growth (the sort that lifts people out of poverty) and bad economic growth (the sort that destroys nature).

Good sorts of productivity improvements increase efficiency, cut costs, and distribute the benefits across society. They often make people redundant, of course, but this is a price worth paying if the economy grows and there are new jobs to replace those being lost within a reasonable time frame.

Bad productivity improvements do much the same: they increase efficiency and cut costs. Where they are bad, however, is if they destroy some public amenity in the process, or if the proceeds are not distributed in a way that creates growth in the economy and new jobs. Improved efficiency is bad if all it does is make a few businesses more profitable while creating unemployment, ruined livelihoods, and social damage.

The coming wave of computerization and robotization generally offers bad productivity improvements. Although it will offer a short-term surge in the output of robotized firms, it will also lead to a drastic cut in the number of people employed by these firms, as well as a sharp decline in the output and employment of firms that do not robotize (because they will no longer be competitive). So many familiar repetitive jobs will simply disappear, leaving only those that require human input or that cannot be mechanized or robotized.

In a few decades, almost everything that can be mass produced will be—both goods and services—so the job market will be dominated by service sector workers, hairdressers, artists, scientists, and gardeners. The jobs of financial analysts, lab technicians, and retail workers will have gone, and the remaining workforce will provide non-robotizable goods and services. At this point, it will be almost impossible to increase the output per worker because most people will work in jobs where this is simply not an option. A gardener cannot weed a garden any quicker; a caregiver cannot look after an elderly patient any faster. The rich world will hit a productivity barrier, in other words, and productivity will gradually stagnate. If the population stagnates at the same time, GDP will no longer increase, because conventional economic growth will gradually approach zero.

In a world dependent on economic growth, that is a very big problem.

Of course, this will not come as a surprise to any economist who has studied productivity carefully in the last half century, because it is the continuation of a trend that started decades ago. The rate of productivity improvement in developed economies has actually been in steady decline since the 1960s.

GRAPH 6: GROWTH IS SLOWING IN THE RICH, BUT NOT IN THE POOR, WORLD

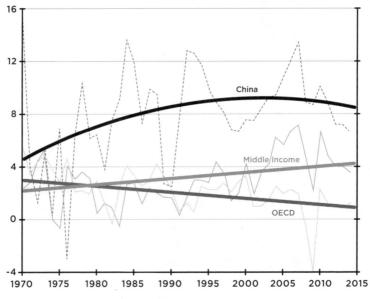

Source: World Bank's World Development Indicators (WDI) via Peter Victor

Scale: Rate of change in GDP-per-person in % per year

The rate of economic growth slows down when societies get richer. The graph (solid grey curve) shows how the growth rate in GDP per inhabitant has declined steadily in the rich (OECD) world since 1970. At the same time, growth rates have been rising in countries that are earlier in their industrialization process, for example China (solid black curve) and the World Bank's middle-income nations (light grey curve).

As you can see in Graph 6, the rate of growth in output per person in the rich world has been in decline for a very long time. This is because the rate of productivity growth—achieved through mechanization, training, and increased use of energy—is slower in the services sector than in agriculture and industry. As the economy shifts further into services, the rate of growth in GDP per person slows. It is simple to increase the output of a farmer by giving him more tractors and fertilizers. It is simple to increase the productivity of factory workers by introducing more machines and energy. And it is possible to increase the productivity of office workers through computerization. But it is extremely difficult to increase the productivity of nurses or artists.

Unfortunately, it is not just the opportunity for further productivity improvements that will slow the rate of growth in the rich world in the coming years. There are three other reasons why conventional economic growth is likely to slow.

They are the subject of the next chapter.

CHAPTER 5

OTHER THREATS TO THE CURRENT ECONOMIC SYSTEM

Aging societies, less accessible resources, and climate change
will add to the current challenges.

W E HAVE ALREADY seen that although the rich world's economic output has increased over the last thirty years, average incomes have stalled, unemployment has risen, and inequalities have widened. And, as we have already also discussed, there is no obvious end in sight to these trends.

As if this were not enough, there are three additional challenges facing the rich world: an aging population, the prospect of some resources becoming more expensive, and climate change. If these are not handled carefully, they will further reduce the pace of consumption growth for the average citizen, as well as the living standards of millions.

To deal intelligently with these challenges requires a change in thinking. Rather than providing lots of goods and services for the young, the economy will need to focus more on the needs of the elderly. Rather than always using the cheapest raw materials, society will be forced to use more expensive, less readily available alternatives. Rather than continuing to rely on emissions-intensive manufacturing, there will be a need to shift to climate-friendly production technologies. These are significant changes, and they are all possible—at least in theory. In practice, however, economic restructuring of this sort tends to be slow and frequently leads to higher unemployment and slower GDP growth during the transition—

neither of which is likely to be embraced with enthusiasm by wider society.

The three biggest hurdles facing the current economic system are as follows:

- **Aging populations.** The average age of people in much of Europe, Japan, and the rest of the rich world (and indeed some parts of the poor world) is rising, tipping the demographic balance. This matters, because older people have different demands and spending patterns.
- **Resource depletion.** Rising resource use, because of rising populations and rising global output, will mean that the price of some raw materials will increase. This will push up the cost of what is consumed, and without a corresponding rise in incomes, the consumption of other goods will fall.
- **Climate change.** Extreme weather events will force governments to allocate more labor and capital to combat their effects.

AGING POPULATIONS

Few people understand the implications of an aging population properly, simply because humanity has almost no experience of this phenomenon, at least outside Japan. When a population ages, large numbers of people who once worked become economically inactive. This has a big impact on government budgets: instead of paying taxes as they once did, these people now receive public pensions, changing a financial inflow to government coffers into a financial outflow. Some elderly people supplement their public pensions with savings or private pensions. A few borrow. But many do not have these options and so have to reduce their spending.

This means that the impact of an aging population is very uncertain, because it is currently unclear whether the elderly of the future will demand more or fewer goods and services than when they worked, though it seems reasonable to think that their consumption will fall.

What is clear, however, is that the composition of total demand in the population will change, because when the proportion of old people increases, the proportion of younger people declines—by mathematical necessity. This fact is illustrated in Graph 7, which shows that the dependency ratio will not rise as fast as many people fear over the coming decades.

GRAPH 7: THE DEPENDENCY RATIO WILL STAY RATHER LOW

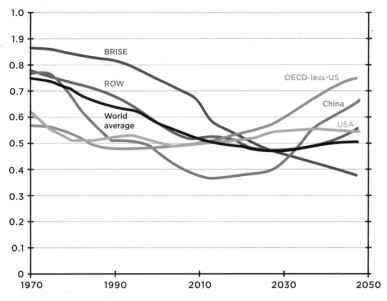

Source: Jorgen Randers, 2052, Chelsea Green, Vermont, 2012

Scale: Number of young plus number of old divided by number of working age

The dependency ratio has fallen in all regions since 1970, because of rapid population growth, and is not expected to start growing again (in some regions) until after 2030, because of slower population growth and more old people.

So, an aging population means that the economy is hit by a double whammy and forced into a transition. There is a need to shift labor and capital into the provision of goods and services for the elderly and out of the provision of goods and services for everyone else.

What is the dependency ratio?

The dependency ratio is the number of people between zero and fifteen years, plus the number of people over sixty-five years, divided by the number of people between fifteen and sixty-five years (the workforce). It is around 0.5 in the rich world, which means each working person has to pay for themselves plus half another person. Or, in less precise terms, each couple must care financially for one child or one elderly person in addition to taking care of themselves, on average.

The dependency ratio is more stable over time than many people think. This is because, when the fraction of old people increases, the fraction of young people declines—given that the sum must be 100%. In the future, the dependency ratio will not increase much (unless there is a major war or a plague), because the increase in the number of old people will largely be compensated for by an almost equal decline in the number of young (see Graph 7).

What is the effect of aging on the economy?

An aging population is one where the average age is rising. It is normally associated with an increase in the proportion of elderly people—typically defined as those over the age of sixty-five.

When people retire, they stop receiving a regular wage, so their consumption depends on new sources of income. Some of their spending is financed by savings or by private investments or pensions, and some by public pensions from the state.

The spending patterns of the elderly are also different. For example, they buy less crockery and fewer airline tickets, and more gardening, medical, and security products. The big question is whether the total demand (per elderly person) will be greater or smaller than when they had jobs. If it is smaller, aging could lead to a decline in overall demand and to a contraction of GDP. The effect may be similar to increasing unemployment. If any decline is not met with increased welfare support, a vicious downwards economic cycle could occur.

From a government finance viewpoint, the problem in many rich-world countries is that the costs of the old are largely paid for by the state, in the form of pensions, elder care, and healthcare. If government finances are to be sustainable when the fraction of old people increases, tax levels on the rest of the population need to rise. This is not an attractive prospect for most people.

These changes bring challenging consequences for businesses, too. If taxes rise, those with jobs have less to spend on conventional consumption,[1] and the growing proportion of elderly citizens reduce their demand for the items they once consumed.

The retired do not need to commute any longer, so they buy fewer train tickets and less gas. They tend to eat less. They do not need pension planning, business lunches, or work clothes. On average, people over sixty-five in the developed world spend 25% less on the things they once consumed but more on healthcare and their families.[2] This trend continues as people get older; by the time people are over the age of eighty-five, their conventional consumption has fallen to half the national average rate.

Compared to the average citizen, the elderly buy 80% fewer tickets for theater shows and the cinema,[3] 67% less crockery, 60% fewer airline tickets, 75% less alcohol, 70% less bathroom linen, and more than 90% less camping equipment. Their spending on cars is half that of the average fifty-year-old. In contrast, spending on eye treatments, lawn care, and security all rise—and substantially so—as does their use of hospitals, healthcare, and home-care services. As much of this is paid for by the state, the total spending of the elderly is usually larger than their "own" consumption, the spending that they finance themselves (for example, their grocery bills).

The crucial point is that the consumption of the elderly is completely different from that of a forty-year-old. Or that of a ten-year-old. The profile of consumers also changes as society gets older, with far fewer men—progressively—than women. This means that not only does the way demand is financed change, the structure of demand changes too, and so aging populations force structural change on the economy.

This change in spending patterns will have more impact in Europe than it currently has in Japan, because many of Europe's future elderly are not going to be very rich. Many people currently in their forties and fifties have not prepared very well for their retirement, in that they have not saved as much as they need to, whereas many of those who have will receive pensions that are far lower than they currently expect because of today's ultra-low interest rates. This means that they will be forced to spend less (because they will have less to spend) and live on whatever they can extract from the state and their families. This will become problematic for the economy if total demand starts declining, if the state and the rich are not willing to give the elderly the purchasing power needed to maintain full employment, or if the next generation is not willing to spend on their elderly parents what they save by having fewer children.

Only 8 million working people in Britain (out of a national population of 60 million) paid into a pension scheme in 2013, one third fewer than sixty years before. The trend is the same in the United States, where the average sixty-five-year-old has only $25,000 in savings.[4]

In Europe, the populations of many countries are also expected to peak in the next decade (in some places they already have), cutting GDP and employment. A declining population does not mean, however, that GDP per head will necessarily fall, or that well-being will decline, as Japan has shown. In spite of a stagnant economy since 1990, the GDP per Japanese citizen has grown nearly as fast as in the United States, because the population has fallen. But there is no guarantee that this pattern will be reproduced in other parts of the world.

In the United States and Australia, countries with younger populations and higher rates of immigration, the prospects for overall GDP growth are better, certainly over the next thirty years or so. The populations of these countries are not yet aging in the same way as in parts of Europe and Japan. This will eventually change, though.

In short, aging populations bring the need for an economic restructuring, as well as increased uncertainty. They bring the prospect of declining overall demand. When populations are aging *and* shrinking, these complexities are multiplied.

Why do people think higher birth rates will solve the aging problem?

Traditionally, parents pay for their children, and the state (and pension funds) pay for the elderly. In the future, parents will have lower costs because they have fewer children than in the past, and the state (and pension funds) will have higher costs because there are more pensioners than before.

The solution is to access the money parents save from having fewer children and spend it on taking care of the elderly. One way to do this is to increase taxes on wage earners. Another way is to keep it all in the family: to expect wage earners to pass on to their elderly parents what they save by having fewer children.

It should come as no surprise that voters dislike the tax increase idea and that many elderly people are uncomfortable about having to rely on the generosity of their children.

Those who call for increased birth rates to solve the aging problem should also think about the effect of this "solution" more. It would take fifteen to twenty years before any newborns entered the workforce. In the meantime, the current workforce would have to pay for both the elderly population and the additional children. Then comes a thirty-to-forty-year period when the solution does work. But that ends when the extra newborns retire (in 2080, say) and further add to the dependency ratio. Mathematically speaking, it would take a continuously rising birth rate to reduce the dependency ratio on a permanent basis. This would create an ever-increasing population and an ever-larger human ecological footprint, which would probably be much more expensive for society in the long term than the small tax rise needed in the short term to pay for the higher proportion of elderly people now.

RESOURCE DEPLETION

Many people do not understand what happens to an economy when the price of a resource starts to rise. Put simply, as the price increases, there is a choice to be made. Either money has to be diverted from something else to pay for the higher cost, or society has to consume less of the resource in question. In the first case, the resource use stays the same (measured in tons per year). In the latter case, society reduces the annual use of the resource.

But in either case, consumption falls, whether it is consumption of the resource itself or consumption of whatever else people formerly spent their money on.

This is important to understand, because there are a number of essential resources that may become more expensive in the years ahead. We will come back to this issue later.

CLIMATE CHANGE

We will discuss global warming in detail in Chapter 7. At this stage, though, it is necessary to understand that climate change will also reduce traditional consumption.

This is because there are two ways in which society can respond to the problem of climate change. People can either stop burning fossil fuels and wait until the effects of what is already in the atmosphere have passed, or they can continue to burn fossil fuels and live with more extreme weather and the problems that brings.

For now, we think that governments and society will continue to choose the second option, largely because it postpones the intro-duction of any unwelcome restructuring, especially of the energy sector.

Another reason why society is likely to decide to live with accelerating climate change is that it generates economic growth. Rebuilding harbors to cope with higher sea levels, reclaiming land swallowed by the seas, and protecting towns from raging bushfires have the curious benefit of generating lots of economic activity. This is not positive activity, of course—and it will gradually eat into the rest of the economy, most of which is currently dedicated to con-sumption. But the repair and adaptation work will create jobs in the short term. Labor and capital will have to be diverted to these environmental repair and rescue missions, and governments will be forced to raise taxes to pay for them. So conventional consumption will shrink, even though the overall scale of the economy will remain the same. Society will effectively substitute the purchase of cars and computers with concrete.

This change is perhaps easier to understand with an exam-ple. When the Dutch need to increase the height of their dikes to withstand climate-induced sea level rises, they will have to employ people to do this work. The work will have to be paid for by the public sector and financed through higher taxes. As the cost will be paid by Dutch taxpayers, it will cut their disposable incomes and so cut their traditional consumption of clothing, electrical equipment, cars, and everything else. If the Dutch still had their old currency, rather than the euro,[5] they could have financed the new dikes by printing money to pay for the work (note that this is not the same as the current policy known as QE, which is the printing of money to generate economic growth and channeling it through the finance sector). Then the cost would have been split evenly among Dutch citizens through higher inflation. The resulting impact would have been the same, though: slightly lower consumption.

The same reasoning applies, incidentally, to all the other "externalized" (see Chapter 9, proposal 8) costs that rich nations have chosen to ignore for so long: the pollution of the waterways and atmosphere, as well as the vast loss of biodiversity and nature. When society eventually decides to deal with these ills, labor and capital will have to be diverted to addressing them, with a consequent reduction in the output of consumer goods and services.

CHAPTER 6

The tools are wrong

DEAD END: THE FAILURE OF
EXTREME FREE-MARKET THINKING

If rich nations continue to fight unemployment and inequality with traditional economic tools, not only will these problems increase, but environmental problems will worsen.

HUMANITY'S BIGGEST PROBLEMS can be categorized as endemic and immediate.

- The endemic problems have endured for years and, in most cases, have become worse.
  - » **Climate change** is the most serious, because without a habitable planet, eventually nothing else really matters.
  - » **Poverty** is a huge problem in both the rich world and the poor world, affecting most of the human population.
  - » **Pollution** has been getting worse, especially in the world's oceans and atmosphere.
  - » **Resource depletion** could slow the pace of human development and lead to conflict.
  - » **Biodiversity loss** appears inconsequential but is not.
  - » **War, terrorism, and conflict** have been increasing, largely because the other problems are not being addressed.
- The immediate problems are largely social or political and tend to get more day-to-day attention. They make it harder for society to address the endemic problems.
  - » **Unemployment** has been getting worse, particularly for the under twenty-fives.

» **Inequality** has been widening, despite decades of economic growth.
» **The pace of economic growth** itself is also seen to be a problem, because it is currently perceived as being too slow (compared to what most people have been told is necessary).
» **Migration** is rising because of conflict, poverty, and, increasingly, climate change.
» **Social friction** is increasing, making extreme political ideas more attractive.
» Finally, **geopolitical friction** is rising, too, pushing the endemic problems further down the agenda or making them worse.

In our view, almost all of these problems are the result of the current economic system. That is, these problems all have the same basic cause—the desire for endless consumption growth without due concern for the effects on the environment and inequality.

As we have already discussed, the current economic system generates constantly rising productivity, and unless it also creates a sufficient number of new jobs, this increases long-term joblessness.

The desire to cut costs and boost short-term profits, driven by the demands of the financial markets, means that real wages have also been declining in many parts of the rich world, with millions of people worse off today than they were thirty years ago.

So today's extreme free-market model is also behind the rise in inequality. The idea of the trickle-down effect, where the wealth of the rich gradually trickles down into the pockets of everyone else, is a myth. The current system achieves exactly the opposite. Those who already have money gain by investing it in the productive economy and resource extraction and receive an income in the form of dividends or asset appreciation. They also make money by lending their wealth to the poor and receiving interest in return. The current system means that wealth is increasingly accumulated by the rich, widening inequalities.

Extreme free-market thinking, driven by an unending desire for increased consumption, is also at the root of the damage humanity is doing to the planet. It is the current economic system that requires the steady rise in the throughput of raw materials. As these are dug up, processed, and used, some of the pollution created causes climate change. According to current thinking, the oceans, forest ecosystems, and polar ice have no economic value beyond the resources they can provide, so the cost of the damage done to them is completely ignored. The rain forests, the world's fish stocks and minerals, are only there to be exploited and used to create value for human society.

So the planet effectively serves the economy, which then rewards the finance system, which then rewards the rich. It is precisely the opposite model that is needed: a system where the finance sector supports the economy, and the economy works for the benefit of the majority of people and in harmony with the planet.

Extreme free-market thinking is greatly responsible for much of the misery in the world, too. Many of the wars in recent decades have been implicitly about access to the resources needed to fuel economic growth, notably oil. The knock-on effects of these conflicts have frequently led to larger and more prolonged wars.

Similarly, many of the migrants across Asia, as well as those from the Middle East and North Africa, are leaving areas not just riven by conflict and ravaged by poverty but also undermined by years of drought and poor harvests, some of which are the direct consequences of the climate change that has been caused by humanity striving for ever-higher economic output.

If things do not change, this trend will accelerate in the future, forcing many more people to move to places where they do not want to go and are unlikely to be welcome.

Extreme free-market thinking has infected society's approach to the world in all sorts of other damaging ways, most of which most people no longer see. Because it promotes individual freedom and consumption at the expense of social cohesion, it has made many people more selfish, greedy, and wastefully materialistic. It has even changed people's views on privacy and consumer protection, because they now think it is better to let companies intrude into their lives or sell them unhealthy products than to be regulated. Minimal intervention in the market is viewed as good, even where there are damaging personal consequences.

It was the craving for economic growth that led to the surge in mortgage lending in the 1990s and to the debt hangover that remains. It led to the sharp increase in U.S. house prices and to the housing bubble in much of Europe a decade ago. Rather than managing this problem before it got out of control, economists persuaded regulators to let the market determine the outcome. So everyone stood back and watched while the bubbles burst. This led to the financial crisis and the subsequent hike in joblessness and human misery. The entire cycle—the housing bubble and the financial crisis—also had exactly the same impact as so many of the other trends we have discussed: it shifted yet more wealth from the poor to the rich.

The current growth-oriented system has put humanity on a vast economic treadmill, in other words, one that moves us ever faster toward a dead end—literally. It appears to be impossible to slow it, because without GDP growth, the system begins to fall apart. But any efforts to intervene, to protect local jobs against low-cost imports, for example, or to take some heat out of the housing market, cause the rate of economic growth to slow. So jobs are lost and inequalities gradually widen. But *boosting* the rate of economic growth leads to exactly the same outcome, with the added problem of greater environmental destruction.

A growing number of people—in academia, in government, even in business—recognize these problems. The Club of Rome correctly anticipated them more than forty-five years ago in *The Limits to Growth*. Often wrongly portrayed as an assault on economic growth, it challenged the growth in resource use and pollution, in the ecological footprint, which threatened to overshoot the sustainable carrying capacity of the planet. The book provided a number of scenarios for global society up to the year 2100, warning that the rapid increase in the ecological footprint risked taking humanity to a very dark place indeed, sometime around the middle of the twenty-first century. At the time the book was first published, in 1972, it was still relatively easy to avoid serious problems. Since then, though, the world has moved into overshoot. So getting out of the mess will be much harder.

Luckily, it is still possible to create a better path forward, as we will explain.

Incidentally, it is worth making clear at this point the fact that so many people are supportive of the extreme free-market model is not an accident, nor is it the result of some natural economic, or human, evolution.

It is by design.

In the 1930s, after the Great Crash of 1929, economists and politicians actually focused their efforts on maintaining full employment, not economic growth. Following World War II, governments focused their policies on job creation, the trade balance, and the value of their currencies. Economic growth was not the main goal then either.

This changed in the late 1970s, when Ronald Reagan and Margaret Thatcher came to power and quickly embraced the ideas of an influential group of economists who had been working together since the late 1940s to change the way people think about economics and society. This group included Friedrich Hayek, Ludwig von Mises, and Chicago School's Milton Friedman, some of the twentieth century's best-known economic thinkers. They were leaders of a group called the Mont Pelerin Society (MPS), established to spread extreme free-market thinking and what they claimed were the "central values" of civilization. Named after the mountain in Switzerland where they first met, members of the MPS saw government expansion, especially of the welfare state, as "dangerous." They saw trade unions as "dangerous," too—and the unregulated market as something close to divine.

Of Reagan's seventy-six economic advisors, twenty-two were members of the MPS. Thatcher's chief economics advisor, as well as many other economists close to her, were members of the MPS, too.

Since then, members of the MPS have actively promoted their extreme free-market ideology throughout the world. They include several past heads of state (Germany, Italy, Czech Republic, Sri Lanka); ministers of finance, economics, and trade (U.K., U.S.,

Belgium, Hong Kong); ex-heads of the U.S. Federal Reserve; members of the U.S. Supreme Court; officials from the Bank of England; a U.S. secretary of state; and nine Nobel laureates in economics. The fact that so many have won a Nobel Prize is no surprise, however. The MPS helped create what is officially called the Nobel Memorial Prize in Economic Sciences specifically to legitimize free-market economic thinking.

Mont Pelerin's members are also responsible for the establishment of a large number of right-leaning and very prominent think tanks that spread free-market economic thinking around the world. Many of these also produce the reports on climate change that deny the scale of the problem or cast doubts about the evidence.

Many prominent journalists are also members of the MPS, including several Pulitzer Prize winners. The society has worked across the world to reform the teaching of economics in universities and to help ensure that the articles published in academic journals support its ideas. In many university economics departments, the free-market model has become the only one that is taught.

The message that these free-market economists promote is both brutal and simple: Governments and individuals should not give money to the needy, because poor people do not spend it properly. It is better to give money to the rich, who will invest it on everyone's behalf, boosting overall output and prosperity.

This worked for a few decades after World War II, but as we have discussed, it has not worked for the last thirty years. Yet millions still believe in it.

The MPS's doctrine is one of perpetual austerity for the majority and perpetual exploitation of the planet, because it is not the role of government to protect vulnerable people or ecosystems. People need to take responsibility for their own lives, and the environment should be protected only if it is profitable to do so. It is up to each individual to find work and to pay for the services they use, such as healthcare and education. People need to save for their futures. It does not matter if many people do not get paid enough to live, or to save, and so have to borrow to consume, or that they are persuaded to borrow beyond their means, or that they cannot afford the medical services they need, or that their education forces them into a lifetime of debt, or that the system fails to provide them with any work, or that they are left abandoned in towns and cities across the world because the company they worked for has relocated to somewhere cheaper and they cannot afford to move or do not want to abandon their families.

Despite all this, many voters in the rich world still enthusiastically support governments that follow these ideas and consequently cut back the welfare systems that protect them and encourage businesses to improve productivity at the cost of their own jobs and living standards.

The extreme free-market model also promotes privatization, another seductively simple but wrongheaded idea. Many people think that businesses should not be run by the state, because they perceive government to be inefficient. And they believe that private enterprise works, because competition, the market, and the profit incentive lead to the best outcome. So businesses, houses, and infrastructure that were once owned by the state, and so the people, are sold—and often at a discount—for a onetime gain. The profits that once went to governments then go to the privately wealthy, while the prices of the goods and services being provided rise, and the number of people employed in these businesses falls, all in the name of efficiency. People then find themselves paying rents to private landlords or incurring higher rail fares or paying new road tolls—not for the good of society or the environment but for the benefit of a small financial elite.

Mainstream economic thinking says that trade barriers should be removed, which seems to be an obviously beneficial idea, too. Adam Smith was, after all, a famous advocate of free trade. Yet, in practice, the mantra of ever-more open markets has become a powerful justification for moving production to those countries with the lowest costs and the weakest employment and environmental regulations.

Just as economic growth does not automatically create jobs or reduce inequality, free trade does not always raise the tide for every boat. Although free-market advocates claim that it promotes growth, this is not always the case. South Korea and Taiwan achieved rapid economic growth for decades by focusing relentlessly on export development, while strictly limiting the flow of imported foreign goods. In contrast, after Mexico joined the North American Free Trade Agreement (NAFTA), its economy stagnated, 28,000 small and medium-sized businesses closed, more than a million farmers gave up their land, real wages fell, and unemployment rose.[1]

Free trade works where there is a balance of opportunity and lots of competition. It is extremely damaging, however, where one side has nothing useful to sell, where there is unfair competition because of subsidies or non-tariff barriers, or where there is blatant exploitation of people, resources, or one country by another. It rarely works for infant strategic industries, such as energy production, capital goods production, car manufacturing, and raw materials extraction, which need protection to grow big enough before they can compete internationally.

Free-market thinking on trade encourages poor countries to sell their resources to rich countries and buy complex manufactured goods in return. So the poor world sells its coal, copper, and timber and is then able to buy cars, medicines, and computers. Rich countries get the resources they need and a market to sell what they manufacture. Poor countries sell their resources and get access to rich-world products in return.

But what if poor countries want to make cars, medicines, and computers themselves? What if they want to build societies based on more than just mining, drilling, and logging? What if they want to provide jobs to locally educated scientists and engineers? With unrestricted trade, establishing their own industrial foundations is almost impossible. Not only do they face resistance from competitors in the rich world anxious to protect their markets, without any scale they cannot make the cars, medicines, and computers as cheaply as industrialized countries.[2]

Unrestricted free trade makes it almost impossible for poor countries to develop. Rather, it forces them to sell their natural resources cheaply and use the revenue for consumption instead of their own industrial development.

The only way to break this cycle is for poor countries to introduce restrictions on imported goods behind which they can establish an industrial base; have their citizens pay more for locally made cars, medicines, and computers for a while; encounter the wrath of foreign competitors; and then open their borders when they are able to compete. This is what China, Japan, and South Korea did in the twentieth century, and with great success. They saw that unrestricted free trade made it impossible for them to build competitive local industries. In restricting foreign competition, they were (and continue to be) accused of protectionism, cheating, and acting unfairly. Yet this approach has also given these countries the strong industrial foundations they have today.

In the last few decades this situation has changed, however, and this approach is much harder for developing countries to take today. Existing and planned global free trade agreements will also expose these countries, their businesses, and their politicians to prosecution if they do anything to disrupt the interests of big global corporations in the future.

It is wrong, then, to claim that open markets are always good and that closed markets are always bad, though this is what the free-market Mont Pelerin–inspired economists have tried to encourage everyone to believe. Like so many modern economic ideas, open markets mostly benefit the rich, those who already have industrial scale and political power.

The demands for more open markets, smaller government, and less regulation have become much more than an economic philosophy, however. Adopted by the United States' political right, fed into the State Department and into the foreign ministries of many European countries, extreme free-market thinking has become a dogma, a tool for the rich world to maintain its position over the poor world. Open your markets and let us in, the rich world says, to stimulate growth and boost living standards—that is, the rich world's living standards, of course.

These free-market ideas have certainly generated lots of economic growth. During the last thirty years, the U.S. economy has more than doubled in size. At the same time, though, the gap between rich and poor has increased dramatically, the prison population has more than trebled, millions more are now unemployed, and one in six people now lives in poverty.[3]

Despite this, only a tiny minority questions the pro-growth agenda.

In truth, it is perfectly possible to live well without conventional economic growth, as we will explain. For this to happen, though, the starting position first has to be acceptable to the majority. The gap between rich and poor has to be narrower than it is now, and everyone needs to have a reasonable source of income.

Before we look at how this can be achieved, we need to add one more ingredient to our complex brew.

CHAPTER 7

THE STORMS AHEAD

Any new approach to economic development must work under the
unsettling climatic conditions that will exist in the future.

"The laws of man and the laws of physics have grown increasingly
divergent, and the laws of physics are not likely to yield."[1]

THE STAGNATION OF rich-world economies and the coming hike
in unemployment because of new technology will arrive at a time
when the world will be changing in many other ways. Thanks to
climate change, one of the ways it will be changing is physically.
Understanding this is important, because the proposals we are going
to make to address the economic and social problems will also slow
the pace of long-term climate change, though they will not stop it.

Most people already have a rudimentary understanding of the
implications of living in a world damaged by global warming. They
understand what rising sea levels, frequent heat waves, and other
sorts of extreme weather might entail. But they seem unable to grasp
what the loss of millions of species of plants and animals will mean,
in much the same way they seem unable to comprehend what it will
mean for someone to take care of all the nuclear waste that humanity
has produced in recent decades, and that will take tens of thousands
of years to decay.

The biggest legacy modern society will leave its grandchildren is
not clever computers and robots, or even vast quantities of wealth

and debt. It is the large and growing level of greenhouse gases in the atmosphere, which are changing the climate of the planet.

Unbelievably, to us at least, twenty-five years after the establishment of the U.N. Intergovernmental Panel on Climate Change (IPCC), there is still lots of debate about climate change, with newspapers and online forums filled with discussions about the causes, the effects, and the trends.

In the scientific community, there is almost no debate. Scientists know exactly what is going on. It is the nonscientists who have the doubts, and it is they who encourage the debates, as well as the think tanks and lobbyists who spread misinformation and uncertainty. They are the ones who give people the hope that they do not need to change their behavior, and businesses the hope that they can carry on polluting.

The facts about what is happening are comparatively simple.[2]

GRAPH 8: GLOBAL ENERGY USE WILL RISE TO A PEAK IN 2040

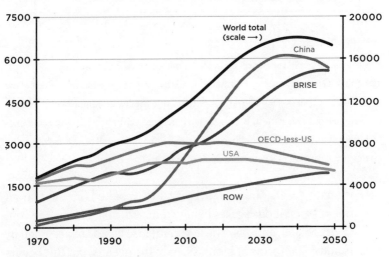

Source: Jorgen Randers, 2052, Chelsea Green, Vermont, 2012

Scale: Energy use in millions of tons of oil equivalents per year

The global use of energy is expected to reach a peak around 2040 and then decline. The rich world is predicted to lead the decline, using ever-less energy from 2020 as a result of slow GDP growth and a continued focus on energy efficiency. The rest of the world—especially China and the fourteen big emerging economies (BRISE)—are expected to show dramatic growth in their annual use of energy.

GRAPH 9: ENERGY USE PER PERSON WILL CONVERGE

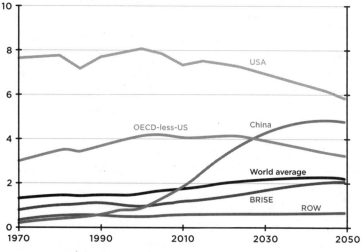

Source: Jorgen Randers, 2052, Chelsea Green, Vermont, 2012

Scale: Energy use in tons of oil equivalents per inhabitant per year

U.S. citizens currently use twice as much energy as the average person in the rest of the rich world (OECD less U.S.). The rest of the rich world uses twice as much as the average Chinese person. This pattern is expected to change toward 2050 because economies will grow at different rates, and because there will be an overall downwards trend in energy use as a result of a continued focus on energy efficiency.

For many years, human activity has resulted in ever-larger quantities of greenhouse gases being produced, mainly from the combustion of coal, oil, and gas. These greenhouse gases are absorbed by forests and other forms of biomass, or in the oceans, but this occurs rather slowly. But because too much gas is being produced today, the system has become overloaded. More gas is being produced than nature can absorb, and the excess is accumulating in the air above us. This traps some of the heat that reradiates from the land and oceans, causing the average surface temperature of the planet to rise.

The main gases that are responsible are carbon dioxide (CO_2), methane (CH_4), and nitrous oxide (N_2O). Increasing quantities of water vapor also play an important role, though they are a consequence, not a cause, of global warming.[3] Water vapor amplifies the effect of the other greenhouse gases and—importantly—will remain in the air until the surface temperature sinks. Which will take a very long time indeed—hundreds of years. The water vapor will be there long after humanity has stopped emitting greenhouse gases, kept in place by its own warming effect.

The gas that is directly responsible for causing most of the heating effect is CO_2, which comes from three main sources. The largest human-made source until comparatively recently was land clearance—cutting down forests and removing other native vegetation. When people destroy plants and forests by burning them or leaving them to rot, the carbon they contain is released in the form of CO_2.

GRAPH 10: GLOBAL CO_2 EMISSIONS WILL PEAK IN 2030

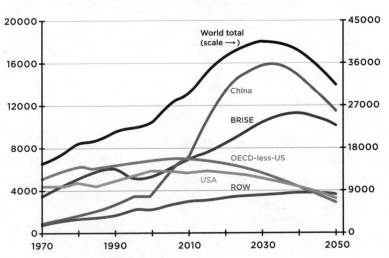

Source: Jorgen Randers, *2052*, Chelsea Green, Vermont, 2012

Scale: Emissions in millions of tons of CO_2 per year

Global emissions of CO_2 are expected to peak around 2030 and then decline. This reflects the pattern of energy use (see Graph 8) and the fact that all regions are expected to gradually move toward less carbon-intensive energy sources, such as solar, wind, hydro, and biomass. The rich world is predicted to lead the process, but in 2050, still more than half of all energy is likely to come from fossil sources.

GRAPH 11: CO$_2$ EMISSIONS PER PERSON WILL FINALLY DECLINE

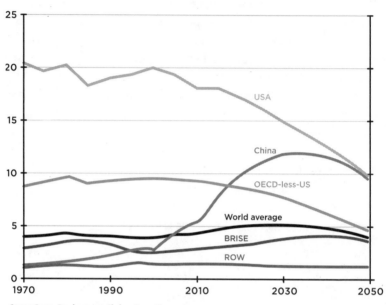

Source: Jorgen Randers, 2052, Chelsea Green, Vermont, 2012

Scale: Emissions in tons of CO$_2$ per inhabitant per year

The amount of CO$_2$ emitted per person is equal to a region's CO$_2$ emissions (see Graph 10) divided by its population (see Graph 1). U.S. citizens currently emit twice as much CO$_2$ as the average person in the rest of the rich world (OECD less U.S.). The latter, in turn, emits twice as much as the average Chinese person. This pattern is expected to change toward 2050 because economies will grow at different rates, and because there will be an overall downwards trend in emissions per unit of energy use as a result of a continued shift toward low-carbon energy sources everywhere.

Fortunately, since it peaked around 1990, and despite the continuing destruction of the rain forests in Brazil, Congo, Indonesia, and many other countries, the quantity of CO$_2$ being released from land clearance has been declining.

CO_2 is also emitted in large volumes during the production of cement, accounting for around 5% of the total. The largest volumes, however, are created when fossil fuels—coal, oil, or gas—are burned as fuel, mostly to generate electricity, for heating, or for transport.

Once it has been released, CO_2 stays in the atmosphere until it is absorbed by plants, through photosynthesis, or by the oceans. Roughly one quarter of the CO_2 emitted by humanity is absorbed by the oceans today, with another quarter taken up by plants. The other half accumulates in the atmosphere, gradually increasing the concentration of CO_2 there and causing global warming. The oceans are absorbing more CO_2 than they did before, leading to acidification of the seas and making life difficult for shell-forming species.

The accumulated effect of human emissions has been to increase the concentration of CO_2 in the atmosphere by more than 40% compared to preindustrial times (around 1750), from 280 parts per million (ppm) to just over 406 ppm today (2016).

Once it is up there, a CO_2 molecule stays in the atmosphere for centuries. This is why the problem will take so long to fix. To shorten the period of a warmer Earth, humanity will need to use extensive carbon capture technology in the second half of the century and actively draw down the CO_2 in the atmosphere. The trouble is this will now require several thousand capture installations around the world, all working full blast for half a century or more.[4]

The next most important gas is methane, which accounts for around a fifth of the warming effect. Methane is released when there is organic decay in environments with too little oxygen—in waste dumps and from animals as they digest their food, for example. It is also released when companies pump oil and mine coal, and accidentally when they produce fossil gas (which is essentially the same as methane).

Methane is roughly twenty times more potent than CO_2, though it stays in the atmosphere for a much shorter time, around ten years, before it is converted to CO_2.

Finally, nitrous oxide—or laughing gas—generates one twentieth of the current warming. It is mostly released because of the degradation of synthetic nitrogen fertilizers from warm and water-logged soils, as well as from streams and rivers where there is agricultural runoff.

Nitrous oxide is even more powerful in its effect than methane and three hundred times more potent than CO_2.[5]

Unfortunately, these greenhouse gases will continue streaming into the atmosphere for decades even after humanity stops creating them. If society stopped using fertilizers tomorrow, for example, nitrous oxide would continue to leak into the atmosphere from the soil for years. The same applies to the methane leaking from landfills.

If humanity continues to emit the gases that are causing global warming at current rates—and the rate of release today is higher than it has ever been—then average global temperatures will rise by 2°C compared to preindustrial times (1750) in about fifty years.[6] By around the middle of the 2030s, the average concentration of CO_2 in the atmosphere will pass 450 ppm, and because of lags in the system, average temperatures across the planet will then hit the 2°C increase some forty years later.

According to the global agreement reached in the COP15 meeting in Copenhagen in 2009, moving beyond a 2°C rise is dangerous because it increases the risk of self-reinforcing runaway climate change. This is when rising temperatures will accelerate larger geophysical changes, such as the melting of the permafrosts or the drying out of the rain forests, which would increase the temperature even more and lead to a chain reaction that would be irreversible in any commonly understood human timescale. Many scientists—supported by the COP21 meeting in Paris in 2015—think even 2°C is too much, however, saying the increase should be capped at 1.5°C. Even at this level, half of the world's coral reefs may die.

Among many other damaging consequences, a temperature increase of more than 2°C could start a runaway melting of the huge Siberian and Canadian permafrosts. This would release vast quantities of methane, further warming the atmosphere and accelerating the melting process. Higher temperatures will accelerate the loss of ice at both poles and the melting of the Greenland ice shelf. This will increase sea levels, adding to the unstoppable rise that has already begun because of the thermal expansion of the top layers (up to 2,300 feet/700 meters deep) of the oceans. But it is important to understand that this process will be extremely slow. It will take a hundred years to increase the sea level by more than 3 feet/1 meter (unless, of course, global society goes totally mad and ignores the need to cut emissions). This is good, of course, because it gives humanity time to act. But it is also bad, because it will take a long time before people experience the damage resulting from their collective inaction.

Because CO_2 stays in the atmosphere for so long, and because it is difficult to collect in sufficient quantities quickly, humanity cannot easily reverse the process it has started. The most people can do at this stage is stop making the situation worse. But even if a humongous program of carbon capture and storage is put in place, it will take more than a century for average global temperatures to return to normal.

A chilling thought in an increasingly warm world.

Part of the problem is that few people understand what an increase of 2°C in average global temperatures actually means. The temperature variations people experience every day are much greater than 2°C, even at the equator. Another couple of degrees seems almost trivial. Can it really be such a problem to increase the global average surface temperature from 13.5°C in 1750 to 15.5°C in 2050?

To understand how big a change this really is, it helps to think about the human body. Like the planet, the human body is a finely tuned biological mechanism that needs to maintain a careful temperature balance. Human body temperatures vary from 37°C by only around half a degree in an average day. A rise of 1°C is classed as a fever. A couple of degrees puts the body at risk.

The average temperature of the planet in 2015 was around 14.5°C, one degree more than in 1750. A further 1°C increase may not sound like much, but it actually takes the planet back to how it was 10 million years ago. A 3°C jump would go back 40 million years, to a time when there was no ice on Earth. If this was to occur again, and all the ice melted (which admittedly would take thousands of years, but still . . .), the sea level would rise by more than 420 feet (130 meters), radically changing life on the planet.

Despite all the evidence of climate change, many people are dismissive. There have been fluctuations in Earth's temperature before, the climate change deniers argue. What is happening is nothing much to worry about, they say, because it is part of a normal cycle. And they say this with confidence, even though they are not well-informed experts in this complex subject.

Unfortunately, these people are mistaken.

It is true that there have been large changes in average temperatures on Earth in a relatively short time throughout history. There were extensive settlements in Greenland for a few centuries, after the eleventh century, during what is known as the Medieval Warm Period. The rivers in Europe regularly froze in the centuries that followed, during what is called the Little Ice Age. And there are Ice Ages every 120,000 years or so. Humanity is actually living near the end of one of the warmer periods—which last up to 10,000 years—that occur every 120,000 years or so, when Earth's distance from the sun is shorter because of the gravitational pull of other planets.

These temperature fluctuations are generally well understood, though. Other influences on the climate are known to be caused by variations in the circulation patterns of the oceans, solar radiation, or volcanic activity. Some changes affect only parts of the planet but not all of it. During the Medieval Warm Period, for example, although it was hotter in the northern hemisphere, it was colder elsewhere. The average temperature across the entire planet was actually little different from that of the twentieth century.

More significantly, science shows that what is happening now, what has been happening over the last fifty years, is not like any of these previous occasions. The speed of change, in both emissions and temperature, and its geographic extent are without precedent. Without an obvious cause, like a volcanic eruption, an abrupt change like this cannot be the result of any natural phenomenon. It can only be the result of human activity.

Scientists know, too, that winters are warming faster than summers, and nights are warming faster than days. There really is more carbon in the trees, in the oceans, and in the air, and this can only be the result of burning fossil fuels. It is also known that there is less heat escaping into space, because a tiny fraction of the incoming solar heat is being trapped.

Today's more optimistic forecasts—based on global society doing only what is profitable to stop what is happening—suggest that human-made emissions will peak just after 2030, and then gradually fall back over the following twenty years to the level they are today. Even then, though, the level of human-made emissions in the atmosphere will be rising. It is just that they will be rising more slowly.

This will result in an increasing frequency of droughts, floods, heat waves, storms, and hurricanes, some of which will be worse than humanity has ever seen. Buildings in many parts of the world will begin to decay, their foundations undermined and their façades weakened by extremes of cold, heat, and humidity that they were not designed to endure. Sea levels will rise, inundating low-lying deltas and many small islands in Asia, thanks to the thermal expansion of water and the steady addition of meltwater from the world's on-land glaciers. Not only will the incidence of air-, insect-, and waterborne diseases increase around the world, they will also appear in places where they were previously unknown. Arctic sea ice will melt, first in summer and eventually all year round. The new weather patterns will also reduce food production in much of the world, as crops are forced to contend with higher temperatures, more rain, and prolonged droughts. Farmers will have to change what they sow and harvest in these regions, and consumers will be forced to change their dietary habits. At the same time, though—to the great pleasure of climate change deniers—food and forests in the temperate north of the planet will grow much better, certainly over the next fifty years.

As many large-scale terrestrial and marine ecosystems will be unable to adapt, hundreds of species of mammals and birds will die out. Thanks to the rise in the CO_2 concentration in the seas, the volume of shell-forming animals in the oceans will sharply decline, too.

The impact of the warming is already visible in Alaska, northern Canada, northern Russia, the Arctic Ocean, and the Antarctic rim. Glaciers are melting, sea ice is retreating more each year, and the permafrost is moving northwards. More densely populated areas have felt the heat, too, notably in the western United States, the Mediterranean, northern Africa, central Asia, eastern Australia, and the tropical forests around the Amazon River. A major worry now is that if the remaining rain forests dry out, they might decay and release even more CO_2, accelerating the warming process.[7]

In some places, the rise in temperatures will be good news—crop yields will improve in high-latitude regions such as Scandinavia, Siberia, and Canada. In other areas, though, it will become too dry, dusty, and hot to grow crops or to live. The availability and quality of water are likely to become problems, too, though these will probably be solvable by increasing water prices and with desalination—which is fine for the rich but will bring additional problems to the poor.

Despite all this, and despite the fact that it is easy to predict these consequences with considerable certainty, we fear that none of this will be sufficiently threatening for humanity to dramatically change its approach to the production of climate gas emissions over the next decade. There will be some progress, of course. There will be a gradual, but slow, move toward low-carbon energy and more energy-efficient production. But this process will be hindered by the fact that most of the changes that need to be made are not profitable from the perspective of the current economic system.

Profit-seeking fossil-based businesses will hinder change, too, and the deniers and doubters will remain vocal enough to drown out the voices of the sane. The short-term nature of humanity, its fear of change, as well as the ongoing love of free-market economics and moneymaking are the reasons. The only hopeful development in this sad story is the fact that solar electricity has finally become cost competitive in sunny climes and so will attract much more investment.

The gradual warming of the world will also change people's outlook. It will make many people nervous and uncertain, less trustful of politicians (who will be seen as even less effective than now), and more fearful about the future. With higher costs to repair climate damage and higher taxes to pay for collective climate adaptation, it will make most people feel poorer, too.

It is in human nature, perhaps, to want short-term fixes to problems, and many people will find it hard to accept that there are none in this case. So there is a risk that people will get angry, too.

The good news is that it is still technically possible to avoid the worst. It is still technically possible to shift to a non-carbon world and keep below the +2°C limit, though this would require immediate and extraordinary action. This is because the solution, though not very expensive in global GDP and employment terms at around 1% a year, still requires a huge change in the structure of the global energy system in a short time. It would need a giant increase in renewable energy investment over many years, which will be opposed vehemently by those currently employed, and invested, in the fossil fuel business.

Unfortunately, for these reasons, we do not believe the necessary steps will be taken in the current economic and political system. Humanity will move steadily toward +2°C, and an era of extreme weather and rising social tension, even though this is perfectly possible to avoid.

A NEW APPROACH

The rich world needs to take a different
approach to economic thinking

What are the main challenges facing the rich world?

The rich world is currently facing five big challenges:
1. A period of robotization, which could increase unemployment and inequality.
2. Aging populations, which are likely to increase government spending or inequality.
3. Harder-to-access resources, which could divert spending away from conventional consumption.
4. Climate change, which will require greater government intervention and progressively higher state spending.
5. Slow productivity growth in those economic sectors where most people will work—namely non-robotizable services, culture, and care—which will reduce the rate of consumption growth that is possible.

If these challenges are met with extreme free-market thinking, the result will be higher unemployment, even greater inequality, accelerating climate change, and, in the long run, lower growth in the consumption per person. In sum, a decline in average well-being.

> The current approach also makes it nearly impossible to deal with climate change and reduce humanity's fossil fuel dependency quickly.
>
> So there is a need for something different, a break with the past. There is a need for governments to plan and to regulate, rather than leaving many important decisions to the vagaries of "the market" and "the invisible hand."

IN PRINCIPLE, IT is simple to overcome the five challenges listed in the box above. To build better societies with smaller ecological footprints, the rich world needs "simply" find a way to:

- stop using coal oil and gas (technically possible but expensive);
- transfer wealth from the rich to the poor (on a continuing basis);
- regulate markets in the interests of the majority and the planet; and
- reduce short-termism, especially within the finance sector.

The problem is that these steps are unrealistic in modern rich-world societies. There would be fierce opposition to them—and this is unlikely to change soon. There is no political majority that favors reducing industrial production, shutting down most of the fossil fuel industry, drastically shrinking and restricting the finance sector, and unraveling some free trade agreements.

There is also no simple, socially acceptable way to reduce the human population, which is also necessary if all earthlings are to enjoy a high material standard of living in the long term.

When it comes to reducing the pace of population growth, all society can do is educate people better (evidence shows that it is especially important to educate young women[1]), boost the incomes of the poor, improve health services, and make contraception more easily available. Without famine, widespread disease, or war, the scale of the human population is a given for the next thirty years. It is almost impossible to change.

What are the obvious solutions to the rich-world challenges?

The obvious (to us, at least) solutions to the five challenges listed in the previous box are to:
1. distribute the benefits of robotization across the whole population,
2. shift enough labor into elderly care,
3. shift enough labor into the supply of climate-friendly resources,
4. transfer a fairer share of the national income to the poor,
5. stop using coal, oil, and gas, and
6. accept that once most people work in non-robotizable services, total income will no longer increase, so further redistribution will be the only way to help the poor.

    If all these steps were taken together, and with the same level of commitment, they would solve the problems of unemployment, inequality, and climate change by allocating jobs and income differently among social groups.

    These steps are not politically feasible, however—and not only because most of them would be fiercely opposed by the rich and powerful. Most are also difficult to implement because they would lead to higher unemployment, or reduced consumption per head, in the short term. In other words, they are impossible because of the short-termism of the market and voters. For any changes to be politically acceptable, the majority of people need a short-term advantage, an incentive.

To most people, it appears as if the only way humanity can shift onto a better path is if a sufficiently large number agree not only on the need for change but also on what is necessary. That would need, among many other things, a huge campaign to get the message out, to help more people understand the need for change. Such a campaign would require the support of the media, without pressure or opposition from corporate and political lobbyists. But more than that, people would have to want to act.

This is not just extremely difficult to pull off; it is, for all practical purposes, impossible.

So, faced with these challenges, the rich world does almost nothing because the mountain appears too big to climb, the task too complex, the goal too imprecise, and the risks along the way too high. Bringing the world back into balance is much more difficult than doing nothing, even though the long-term consequences are dire. Voters and politicians fear the fallout of change, the social turmoil, and the job losses during the transition. They worry that living standards will decline in the short term.

Throughout history, those who oppose or fear the prospect of momentous change tend to fight, and even those who support it are unsure, because they are unclear on what the outcome might be.

Moreover, it seems that most people do not really want to be altruistic so that others might benefit from what they do. Few are genuinely willing to make a sacrifice today, even if it is for the benefit of their own grandchildren. This is why we chose not to call this book *Your Kids and How Not to Kill Them*—which was one of our early ideas.

Which criteria need to be met to move forward and address the challenges?

There is a need to find a way forward that:
1. does not cost more, in the short term, than doing nothing,
2. does not lead to higher unemployment and greater inequality in the short term,
3. helps to turn the political system and leadership in a better direction,
4. does not cause the existing system to collapse or stumble,
5. builds a wider awareness about the extent of the changes needed,

6. is welcomed by the democratic majority, if not the 99%,

7. offers immediate benefits for most people, and

8. moves humanity toward a better and more sustainable future, with a lower ecological footprint per person.

Only when most of these conditions are satisfied will it be possible to move forward.

The governments of rich-world societies are unable to apply the six obvious solutions to the five challenges because they entail short-term costs for a long-term benefit—a benefit that may not come during the lifetime of those making the sacrifice.

Fortunately, there are a number of alternative and unconventional policies that can achieve the same ends. They offer immediate benefits to the majority, which should make them politically feasible, and address the five challenges progressively. They also reduce unemployment and inequality, while slowing the pace of climate change.

We admit, right here right now, that our proposals are far from ideal. By necessity, they are indirect, and hence difficult to explain, even to those who are positively inclined toward doing whatever it takes to bring about change for the better. It will also take time for their impact to be felt. And they violate some of the central ideas of free-market economics. They will, however, move the rich world in a better direction, and they should be politically acceptable to the majority.

Our proposals introduce a deliberate deviation from today's extreme free-market thinking but without undermining the entire system. They gradually shift rich-world economies onto a more sustainable path, slowing today's growth-driven treadmill enough for global society to get off. They also ensure that rich nations' economies are built according to a plan that benefits the majority and does not simply maximize the short-term profit of a few.

In the rich world today, the main reason to continue to increase production and consumption is that this is what is needed to avoid a collapse of the economic system. (You might want to read that sentence again.) It is also what the financial system demands.

Yet the developed world does not need more wealth or more goods. As Keynes anticipated, there are already enough of these. The problem is one of distribution. What rich-world societies need most of all is to redistribute work, wealth, and incomes so that everyone receives a fairer share.

In the developing world, the situation is different, and there is still a need for conventional economic growth. We will discuss this in more detail in Chapter 11.

What does it take to build a better world?

We have already listed the five challenges facing the rich world, the six obvious solutions, and the eight conditions that need to be satisfied to make these solutions politically feasible. But what does it take to build a better world?

- An economy with much lower materials throughput. This does not mean that the GDP has to be smaller. In fact, it will probably grow, because the value of many existing economic activities will increase and many new sorts of economic activities will emerge—in environmental protection, resource efficiency, research, culture, and care, for example.
- A human ecological footprint below the sustainable carrying capacity of the planet. Although the human economy—the GDP—can continue to grow, the human footprint cannot. It needs to decline. Humanity's extraction of resources, production of emissions, and destruction of biodiversity has to fall, and sharply. This is most obvious in the area of human-made greenhouse gas emissions.
- Sufficient redistribution of income so that everyone has enough to live comfortably. The quickest way to achieve this would be to provide a lifelong guaranteed livable income to everyone, as a basic human right, paid for by the state. (We will explain later why this is not actually possible, unfortunately—though much can be achieved.)

- A means of ensuring that everyone has a job or meaningful purpose in life. This requires a redefinition of paid work.
- A regulatory and political mechanism to make all this happen.
- An economic system that can organize and pay for the collective action needed to respond to climate change and the other threats to human well-being.
- A way to measure subjective well-being and ensure that society is on the right path.

Thankfully, most of what is needed to make the transition is technically possible. It is possible to reduce damaging emissions without serious consequences for jobs and inequality. It is possible to use taxes and incentives to redistribute incomes. It is possible to create enough purpose and guarantee sufficient income for everyone.

In the next chapter, we offer thirteen unconventional, sometimes controversial, but politically feasible proposals to make the changes needed.

CHAPTER 9

THIRTEEN POLITICALLY FEASIBLE PROPOSALS TO REDUCE UNEMPLOYMENT, INEQUALITY, AND CLIMATE CHANGE

A more realistic way to create a better world is to redistribute income and work to reduce the collective ecological footprint. There will be opposition from business and finance, but if governments introduce policies that provide short-term benefits for the majority, more people will gain than lose.

TO RECAP: FOR most of the last thirty years, unemployment has been rising in the rich world, while the gap between rich and poor has been widening. This is not what conventional economists said should happen. They said that the strong economic growth experienced from 1980 onwards should have created jobs and spread the wealth around more evenly, especially as it was supplemented by open trade and less market regulation. Instead, average standards of living have stagnated or declined in much of the developed world. Only the rich have become richer, while poverty has increased. Now, thanks to new technology, even more jobs are at risk.

These problems have also made it hard to solve the big environmental challenges of pollution, resource depletion, species loss, and climate damage—because many people think that whatever is done to respond to these problems will result in slower growth, further job losses, and even wider inequality.

Yet to continue on the current path makes no sense. Eventually, the widening gap between rich and poor will undermine social stability. Sticking with the current system will also ruin the planet for future generations, because further conventional economic growth will require more fossil energy, which will result in more of the damaging emissions that cause climate change.

For most of the rich world, the option of continuing along the path of rapid GDP growth no longer exists in any case, because the rate of productivity growth in everything that cannot be mechanized or computerized will continue to slow, no matter what economists and politicians do. The populations of Europe and Japan are going to decline, which means fewer consumers, which in turn means fewer producers. Although the coming wave of new technology will boost productivity growth for those who still have jobs, once everything that can be robotized has been, there will be very little scope for further productivity improvement, because most people will work in non-robotizable services, culture, and care. In these sectors, productivity growth is very slow and often undesirable. So in the postindustrial, post-robotized economy, there will be very little scope for any further economic growth. Not only will the population of many countries be in decline, the average GDP per person will stagnate.

So there will be a general freezing of the system, irrespective of how much interest rates are cut, workers are reeducated, or money is printed. At the same time, governments will have to spend more on responding to the effects of climate change, forcing them to raise taxes. This will take workers and investment away from the consumer goods sectors and slow consumption growth. Some raw materials will become more expensive, too, and more effort will be required to maintain an acceptable flow of resources, which in turn will result in less capacity for consumption growth.

As we discussed in earlier chapters, fixing these problems is not going to be possible using conventional ideas within the existing economic system. There is a need for some new thinking, for an alternative to the extreme free-market ideology. Unemployment and inequality have to be attacked head on, not indirectly by promoting conventional economic growth. And we know that for any new policy to work, it must benefit the democratic majority in the short term, because that is what motivates people to vote for, and then demand, change.

To this end, we offer thirteen politically feasible proposals to improve average well-being in the rich world. Our goal is a future where average living standards will be higher than if extreme free-market thinking is allowed to continue. We believe that by combining our thirteen proposals—by grafting them onto the current free-market system—it is possible to steer the rich world toward a better future, to counter the five challenges (see Box: What are the main challenges facing the rich world? in Chapter 8), and, most importantly, to reduce future unemployment, inequality, and climate change. Almost all of our ideas will need to be implemented gradually, over many years if not several decades.

Thirteen proposals to reduce unemployment, inequality, and climate change

1. **Shorten the length of the work year** to give everyone more leisure time.
2. **Raise the retirement age** to help the elderly provide for themselves for as long as they want.
3. **Redefine "paid work"** to cover those who care for others at home.
4. **Increase unemployment benefits** to maintain demand during the transition.
5. **Increase the taxation of corporations and the rich** to redistribute profits, especially from robotization.
6. **Expand the use of green stimulus packages by printing money or raising taxes** to help governments respond to climate change and the need for redistribution.
7. **Tax fossil energy and return the proceeds in equal amounts to all citizens** to make low-carbon energy more competitive.
8. **Shift taxes from employment to emissions and resource use** to reduce the ecological footprint, protect jobs, and cut raw materials use.

9. **Increase death taxes** to reduce inequality and philanthropy while boosting government income:
10. **Encourage unionization** to boost incomes and reduce exploitation.
11. **Restrict trade where necessary** to protect jobs, improve well-being, and help the environment.
12. **Encourage smaller families** to reduce the pressure of humanity on the planet.
13. **Introduce a guaranteed livable income for those who need it most** and give everyone peace of mind.

Of course, this may seem like an idealized list that has absolutely no chance of being accepted by those in power—by which we mean financiers, the rich, and big corporations, not elected politicians. Many of our proposals will also be resisted by those who fear losing their jobs or paying more tax. But notice that we have deliberately listed proposals that we believe have a chance of being politically accepted in the rich world. This is because each of our proposals, with the exception of number 12, will provide an immediate benefit to most people. They should appeal to the democratic majority of voters, which in most of the rich world still carries enough weight to get legislation passed—though we acknowledge that this can take time.

Later, we will examine some of the hurdles that need to be overcome for these changes to be adopted. In the meantime, we will explain our proposals one by one.

1. SHORTEN THE LENGTH OF THE WORKING YEAR

Our first proposal secures a fairer division of national income among citizens. Instead of 90% of the population working full time and receiving, say, $30,000 a year each, our ambition is for 100% of the population to work, each receiving $27,000 a year. The main benefits of spreading paid work among those who want it would be:

- reduced unemployment,
- reduced inequality, and
- increased flexibility to slow the pace of climate change.

What are the effects of shortening the work year?

Every year, a certain amount of work needs to be done in an economy. Ideally, everyone would take part in this work and receive their share of the total output. (Notice that we focus here on paid work, not uncompensated activities, even though these take up a lot of time for many people.)

Full employment can be achieved simply, by splitting all the work that needs to be done among all those who want to work. If there is not enough work for everyone to work full time, it makes sense to reduce the number of hours worked per person per year (i.e., having 100% of the working-age population working 90% of the time, rather than having 10% of the working-age population unemployed and the rest working full time). So if there is unemployment at the outset, the total cost of an organized shortening of the work year is zero. The policy simply shifts the total effort and rewards of work across the population.

Still, many people who have full-time jobs will oppose the shortening of the work year. They will not necessarily want to give part of their income to the previously unemployed. But the policy could be reengineered to garner majority support. It could be introduced gradually as a legislated increase in the number of annual vacation days (e.g., two more days of vacation every year with no reduction in pay).

Were such a policy to be introduced in the United States, after twenty-five (!) years, Americans (who currently work 2,000 hours per year in a full-time job) would work as little as Germans (who currently work 1,600 hours per year). The total effect of "more compulsory vacation" would be lower growth in GDP,

> consumption, and resource use and more time for everything
> else—family, friends, and hobbies.
>   However, if there is full employment at the outset, any short-
> ening of the work year comes at the cost of reduced output
> growth. In that case, it will amount to choosing lower production
> (and consumption) growth in return for increased leisure time.
> Many nations have done this over the past thirty years, taking
> some of the productivity growth as increased wages and some as
> more vacation.

The first problem with this proposal is that many fully employed people do not want to reduce their working time and income—even if they are offered increased leisure time. The second problem is that there are practical difficulties in having many people sharing what was formerly one job. The third problem is that it will be difficult to make sure that people do not work longer hours than allowed.

As we will explain, these problems are real but solvable, particularly if the length of the maximum work year is reduced slowly—for example, by increasing the number of vacation days by one or two a year.

There is an additional advantage to reducing the length of the maximum work year, or increasing the minimum number of vacation days. More leisure time will slow the growth in the human ecological footprint. Instead of spending time producing, with the associated use of resources and pollution, people will enjoy more leisure time. And, importantly, this added leisure time will not lead to increased spending, since the total national income will remain constant. Of course, with more leisure time, there is a risk that people will take the chance to jet off on vacation, increasing their carbon footprint and making the environmental situation worse. This should not stop governments from reducing the length of the work year, however. Rather, they should make the change that is needed to gradually shift the economic system onto a more sustainable path first, and then deal with any unwanted consequences. We will come back to this issue later.

The losers of this policy are those who only want the opportunity to make as much money as possible. But since that group is the minority, the majority of voters/workers should be able to pass the necessary legislation to protect themselves from those few whose only purpose in life is to make money.

Let us look at the details.

Logically, if decently paid work is scarce and set to become scarcer, if GDP growth is low and likely to move toward zero, and society wants to reduce inequality, the solution lies in organizing the economy so that work and income are more evenly distributed. The economic structure needs to be changed so that each person receives something closer to a fair share of the total annual output.

The basic equation here is easy to understand. Taking the GDP of an average rich-world country and dividing it by the population provides a good estimate of the average gross income per person. In Germany, this was just over $35,000 in 2005 U.S. dollars PPP,[1] and in the United States it was more than $40,000. Even in the poorer parts of the developed world, such as Romania or Bulgaria, it works out to more than $15,000. (Note that these numbers are per inhabitant, not per worker. So a family of four produces an annual value of four times these numbers—that is, $60,000 per year per family, even in the poorer European nations.)

So, in theory, there is enough income in every rich-world country for people to live reasonably well. There is even space for some level of inequality, allowing those who take on bigger responsibilities to be paid better than average. If all the paid work in these countries could be redistributed in some way, no one would need to worry about unemployment or not having enough income to live. And no one would have to toil for more than the prescribed number of hours each year. Everyone would get a reasonable share of the available work and everyone would get a reasonable share of the national income.

The problem is how to achieve this, especially as some people—mostly those who currently earn the highest incomes—would lose out.

Our proposal is for societies to move toward a fairer system gradually, by slowly reducing the *maximum* amount of paid work allowed per person (per week/month/year) so that there is a gradual decrease in the *average* amount of paid work done per person. By doing this slowly, the system and society will have time to adapt.

Let us explain in more detail.

In most rich-world countries, the share of the population that has a job, or wants to work, is typically just under half the total. In the United States, for example, the civilian labor force is 155 million people out of a population of 320 million.[2] Within that labor force, just under 120 million are currently working full time, just over 27 million work part time, and 8 million are unemployed.[3]

Assuming the 120 million full-time employees work 40 hours a week and the 27 million part-timers work 20 hours a week, they work a total of 5,340 million hours a week. If this is divided equally across the civilian work force, then each person has to work only 34 hours per week (5,340 million hours a week/155 million people).

In other words, the United States can create full employment by reducing the amount of work done by the 120 million people currently in full-time employment by 15%, from 40 hours a week to 34 hours a week—or, more realistically, from 2,000 hours a year to 1,700 hours a year.[4] This would create sufficient paid job openings to employ all 155 million people full time (which, to be precise, would allow each person to work 1,700 hours a year, compared to 2,000 hours a year today). Then, without any economic growth at all, there would be enough paid work for everyone. Not only would everyone have a full-time job, but they would also have more leisure time, on average.

Imagine it like this (this example is greatly simplified to explain our thinking): A farmer wants to hire people to pick apples at harvest time and gets one hundred applicants. He can either employ eighty full time and ten part time, leaving ten without any work, or he can employ all of them, have them all work slightly shorter hours, and achieve exactly the same result for him at the same cost. Then everyone would have money to buy the cider he produces, and most would have more time to consume it. Moreover, if they were thirsty enough, and spent all of their income on his cider, he would sell exactly the same amount whether he employed eighty people or one hundred. This means that the GDP (output) is the same, regardless of how many people are employed. The problem is, of course, that each of the hundred people will have a slightly lower income than each of the eighty would have had.

But this may be a surmountable problem in the rich world, where the average income is already high enough to satisfy most ordinary needs. Also, much of the pressure for higher wages is not because the majority of people actually need a higher income, but because they want to keep up with their neighbors.

Legislating a maximum length for the work year—or, to put it more attractively, increasing the minimum vacation days a year— should be a welcome option for hundreds of millions of people throughout the rich world. Most of those employed in full-time jobs will be able to work less and have more free time, and all (well, almost all) those who are unemployed today will have the chance to find a job and the opportunity to earn a decent income, regain their self-respect, and have a sense of purpose.

How is it possible to make this transition without causing major disruption to society?

One way to implement a shortening of the maximum working year is to slowly increase paid vacation time, as we mentioned earlier. Another is to gradually reduce the length of the workweek. In practical terms, the former is simpler, because even a small reduction in the length of the working week can be complicated for businesses to manage.

If Congress gradually increased the average paid vacation time of U.S. employees (which was just under eight days a year per person in 2014) to the level that currently exists in Germany (around thirty days a year, excluding paid public holidays), this would reduce the length of the average American's work year by around 10%. That would be enough to employ most of those who are currently working part time or are unemployed. Again, we hasten to point out that resistance to this move would be fierce, especially among the country's business owners and the rich—after all, they would appear to be shouldering the bulk of the financial burden that comes with increased paid vacation time. But remember that this is only in the short term; in the long run, the cost increase will be passed on to consumers, who will carry the cost through higher prices in exchange for more leisure.

Many rich countries have already systematically and successfully shortened the work year. In Norway, for example, the number of hours worked in a full-time job has decreased steadily since the 1970s, from around 1,800 to 1,400 hours a year. Yet labor productivity has risen steadily, so much so that if Norwegians had followed the U.S. model with longer hours and less vacation time, their annual incomes would have been 30% higher today. But they chose a different path. Today, few Norwegians believe that they would be happier if they had less leisure time and more money.

Similarly, unions in Denmark were once asked to choose between a 3% wage rise and 3% fewer workdays. They overwhelmingly voted for the latter, because more leisure makes sense in a rich country. In this case, note that the pay per year would stay the same, but the pay per hour worked would increase by the traditional 3%.

Even Germany has followed this strategy and reduced the length of the normal work year from 2,000 to 1,600 hours a year over the last fifty years. It made the transition by gradually increasing paid vacation days and simultaneously reducing the length of the working week over several decades (but doing it in the same way as Norway, so slowly that there was still room for some increase in annual salaries).

In the United States, where there is no statutory minimum paid vacation time, our proposal would need legislation, so the change would be something of a challenge in the current political climate. But we hope that our proposal would attract popular support, as it is in the interests of the majority of people.

Of course, our critics might point to France, where there has been a thirty-five-hour workweek for nearly twenty years, but many people view the policy as a failure because it has not reduced unemployment. To this we have three responses. First, those who deem the French policy a failure are typically business owners and those on the political right, whereas those who support it tend to be workers and those on the political left. So much of the criticism is the result of vested interests. Second, as well as lacking popular support, the French government tried to introduce the reduced working hours too quickly. We propose that the change be introduced gradually, over twenty years or more, so that everyone has time to adapt. Finally, and most importantly, the French have not increased the retirement age sufficiently to compensate for the shorter working week. Instead, many people now work shorter hours and then retire much earlier, too, increasing their burden on the state. This partly explains why our second proposal is to increase the pension age (see below).

So how would society pay for the transition to a shorter working year? The answer depends on the conditions that exist when the policy is introduced.

If there is unemployment at the outset, the "winners" will be the formerly unemployed, because they get a job and an income. The "losers" will be the formerly employed, because they will have to give away part of their income in return for more leisure. Alternatively, if there is full employment at the outset, the cost of increased leisure will be borne by everyone collectively.

If working hours are reduced without a drop in pay, business owners will pass the cost on to consumers in the form of higher prices. This will somewhat reduce the amount of goods and services consumed. If, however, the additional vacation days are matched by a proportional cut in pay, wage earners will carry the cost directly and be forced to reduce their consumption.

In either case, the majority pays the bill—in the form of reduced consumption growth. But they will also enjoy increased leisure time.

The system is flexible. If workers are replaced by machines and robots over the next twenty years at the rate many people anticipate, the model can be adapted from year to year to maintain full employment and ensure that everyone has a job and enough money to live.

No one would need to worry about the threat of unemployment, even if total production (GDP) declines.

Of course, some people may see a limit on the number of paid working hours as an unwelcome restriction on their personal freedom. This is why it is probably better to fund the system by making employers maintain pay levels in the short term and pass the costs on to their customers. People are more likely to accept a law that offers more time off for the same annual salary. (It would be possible to pass on the costs, despite competition, because all businesses would face the same increase in hourly labor costs.)

Regulations concerning maximum work hours would primarily affect larger businesses, which are more likely to follow national labor legislation, of course. So a final question is how would our proposal to shorten the work year affect small businesses and the self-employed? The short answer is that small businesses and the self-employed will have a choice. They can choose to either look for a safe job in a big organization, with a guaranteed income and rising leisure time, or go it alone and work for as many hours as it takes to accumulate their desired level of income. For this to work, it would need to be illegal for big companies to outsource permanent tasks to self-employed individuals or small businesses. It would also need to be statutory for self-employed people to charge their clients an hourly rate that covers their full health insurance and pension plan costs.

Those who go it alone could then choose to take as much vacation as everyone else or work as hard as they wish. If a large number chose the latter course, then the impact of our first proposal would be weakened. But lessons from very rich countries indicate that this group is small, and the inclination to take time off is strongly affected by what people's neighbors do. If big organizations are forced to hire full-time staff to do the work they currently outsource, then self-employed life may become so uncertain that many will forgo the dream in exchange for a steady income, combined with ever more leisure.

Those wanting to work more should keep in mind that it is actually healthier to work less. A study of more than 600,000 men and women from across Europe, the United States, and Australia published in *The Lancet* in 2015 found that those working fifty-five hours or more per week had a 33% higher risk of stroke than those working a thirty-five-to-forty-hour week. Longer hours also bring a 13% increased risk of developing coronary heart disease.[5]

In some parts of Europe, even in some of the most economically successful countries, it is already extremely difficult to set up a one-person business. The state actively discourages it by expecting the self-employed to pay fully into the social security system from day one. Those who want to work for themselves have to pay much the same monthly healthcare contribution as those working for big firms, which is only fair because they will one day require the same care. The same goes for payments into a pension fund, which is also required by law. Some governments also make it difficult for self-employed people to save much on their tax bill, one of the main benefits for those who are self-employed in the most laissez-faire nations.

This is a reversal of the thinking that has become commonplace in countries such as the United States and the U.K., where self-employment is promoted as reflecting the apparent desire of many people to become entrepreneurs, to gain more personal freedom. Yet much of this notion is wrongheaded, driven by the lobbying power of big businesses who want to save money rather than by the dreams of millions of individuals, many of whom become trapped in unstable, poorly paid jobs that they do not enjoy very much.

Uber drivers, for example, are mostly self-employed. They work the number of hours they choose, and because they are not Uber employees, Uber does not need to pay them during their vacations, contribute to their pensions, or pay much in the way of other social security taxes on their behalf. These responsibilities are effectively socialized, paid by society as welfare, saving Uber money. This is partly what allows the company to offer a cheaper transportation service.

It is up to the drivers to decide to plan for their future, to pay for their own health insurance, and to cover their living costs if they cannot find enough work.

What companies like Uber are doing is cutting their costs to compete more effectively and pushing a large part of the usual social costs (pension, health insurance, unemployment benefits) of employing people onto the individuals, their families, and the rest of society. Their drivers will still need as much medical care one day as anyone else, and they will still need to have an income when they are old or unable to work. By encouraging their drivers to be self-employed, though, Uber takes no responsibility for these costs (as traditional taxi firms must).

In such cases and many others, self-employment should be discouraged, partly to ensure that there is a level playing field for all employers, and also that there is fair competition, so that some businesses cannot save money at the cost of wider society.

Reducing the length of the work year can also help reduce the pace of human ecological destruction.

As we have already discussed, the annual production of a nation (its GDP) can be viewed as the number of workers multiplied by the output per worker per year. The output per worker per year is the number of hours worked each year multiplied by their output per hour worked. So if the average number of hours worked per year is cut by more than the population growth rate, the result would be a decline in GDP (relative to what it would otherwise have been) and, ultimately, a reduced human ecological footprint. People could have more vacation, spend less time at work, and also enjoy the benefit of less environmental destruction.

What would people in the rich world do if they had to spend more time away from the office or the factory floor?

We believe that they would gradually do all the things that they currently dream about doing: spending more time with their family, more time on hobbies, more time enjoying themselves. As the amount of leisure time increased, they would start doing themselves what many of them currently pay other people to do: cooking food, maintaining their home, and providing care. If this structural shift went so far as to generate unemployment in the restaurant, maintenance, and care sectors, this could be handled by deeper cuts in the maximum amount of paid hours per person per year. The limited amount of available (paid) work should still be split evenly among citizens. Instead of having some people unemployed, all would be working and having longer vacations than they do now.

More compulsory vacation and a shorter working year is a good solution to the problem of unemployment in the rich world, especially when rich nations face slower GDP growth. It greatly reduces inequality and even helps cut humanity's environmental impact. It is also likely to be appreciated by the majority of the population. So it meets our criteria for a successful unconventional policy intervention that offers immediate benefits to most people.

2. RAISE THE RETIREMENT AGE

Our second proposal for a more sustainable economic system involves raising the retirement age in the rich world. This allows more people to continue to work and provide for themselves for longer and reduces their burden on the state.

What are the effects of increasing the pension age?

Increasing the pension age reduces the dependency ratio in an economy. It makes it easier for those with jobs to pay for all the young and old. It is a very powerful policy handle, because it only takes a small increase in the pension age to reduce the dependency ratio significantly. If the pension age were increased by just a few years in rich countries, the dependency ratio would fall by more than it is expected to rise in the next twenty years under current policies. Similarly, if the pension age were increased from age sixty-five to age seventy, societies could eliminate the rise in the dependency ratio expected from a declining population.

As long as it does not lead to more unemployment, raising the pension age increases the size of the workforce and boosts GDP, as well as GDP per inhabitant (as long as the population does not increase). It increases output, and so consumption (but also the ecological footprint). It can also reduce inequality, if average wages are higher than average pensions.

There are two objections commonly raised against the idea of increasing the pension age.

The first is that many older people may not be able, or want, to work beyond the traditional pension age. The solution is to allow people to choose between retiring early on a lower pension or later with a higher pension. The accumulated cost to the state (or pension fund) over the life of the pensioner should be the same. A second solution is to allow for a transition, with a shorter work year (and lower annual income) for any older people who want it.

The second objection to the idea of a higher pension age is that it steals jobs from the young. This is true if total demand remains constant. But demand will not remain constant if older workers make more money. Then there will be more demand for the type of things that they buy: culture, travel, healthcare, etc. And even if demand stagnates and unemployment rises, this can be fixed by reducing the length of the working year.

In the last few decades, most of the developed world has moved from having a reasonably sustainable demographic pensions balance, where there were a manageable number of older people who required to be paid for a manageable number of years of retirement from pension systems that were (mostly) adequately funded, to one where there is a large and growing number of old people who frequently retire earlier and live much longer than before, and who depend on pension systems that are mostly underfunded, thanks partly to the financial crisis as well as to a change in social attitudes that has led many people to spurn the idea of saving.

In Europe, in 1900, those who were entitled to a pension would get their first payment at age sixty-five.[6] This was the statutory retirement age. Few people received any payments, though, because the average life expectancy at the time was only forty-four. A century later, in 2000, the retirement age was still sixty-five, but average life expectancies had risen to seventy-four. So rather than pensions being paid to a small minority of the elderly population, they are now paid to the majority.

Many believe this situation is made worse by lower birth rates today, because there are progressively fewer younger people who are able to pay for any shortfall in the savings of the elderly. In 1960, in the United States, each person in retirement was supported by just over five working people, spreading the load of the pension payments (much of which came not from a pot of money that had been saved and invested but from income taxes).

By 2030, this ratio will be one pensioner for just over two working people, a rather more difficult equation.[7] But as we discussed in Chapter 5, this is not the fundamental problem, because when the proportion of elderly increases, the proportion of young declines (see Graph 7). Although workers must pay more for the costs of those who have retired, they save by having to pay for fewer children. The difficulty arises because the costs of children in modern societies are largely paid for by their families, whereas the pensions and healthcare costs of the elderly are largely paid for by the state (or pension funds). So aging societies require tax increases, taking whatever workers save by having fewer children and giving the money to the old.

Higher healthcare costs and unrealistic expectations on the part of many middle-aged people about what they might expect to get paid in old age are also a problem. In the U.K., and some other countries, there are two additional difficulties. First, many people apparently do not understand the pension system properly and think they do not need to save until they are relatively old.[8] And second, the government currently allows people to withdraw everything they have saved for retirement whenever they wish and then spend it, rather than drawing it down gradually during their years as pensioners. This means there is a growing risk that those who withdraw their pensions early and spend them quickly will end up costing the state more in the future—or will live miserable lives without any money in their old age.

These pension problems exist in both the private and the public sectors, for those who worked for companies or government in some form, and in most countries within the OECD. Without a change in the legislation concerning the retirement age, millions of people risk being unable to maintain their standard of living while being forbidden to work by the currently legislated retirement age.

By combining our first two proposals, and adding one that boosts the income of those who are temporarily unemployed (which we will discuss next), we believe it is possible to ensure that everyone who is able to work can find enough to do, and those who do not will have a large enough income to live.

We also believe it will be politically feasible to pass legislation to increase the pension age. The vast majority of voters will see this as a relief, as a postponement of the time when they will have to spend even more money on their elderly parents.

3. REDEFINE PAID WORK TO COVER THOSE WHO CARE FOR OTHERS AT HOME

What are the effects of converting voluntary work to paid work?

Consider two working-age people. One cares for an elderly parent at home; the other works in a nursing home. One is unpaid and the other is paid, yet they both do the same work. What happens if society pays home carers for their work?

The first effect is to increase GDP, because society now includes the value added by the home carer. This leads to an increase in the GDP per person. The second effect is an increase in the number of paid jobs, and in the percentage of people registered for work (the labor participation rate). Third, paying people for what they once did for free redistributes income. It also redistributes economic power, allowing those who are currently unpaid to express their own economic wishes directly, not through the income of another.

In summary, there is little change in the underlying human reality, as the same work gets done. There is, however, a significant change in GDP, GDP per person, jobs, labor participation, and income distribution.

As we have already discussed, one of the major benefits of the period of rapid economic growth after World War II was that many more women entered the workforce. It gave a larger share of the population the opportunity to earn an income and did much to boost gender equality.

The economic consequences of this change were curious, however. Although millions of women gave up doing the laundry, or caring for children and the elderly at home, many ended up doing exactly the same work as employees—working in laundries, kindergartens, and hospitals. Offering women a way out of the home led to a near doubling of GDP in many countries, yet there was little change in the availability of many vital services. The change gave more women an income, greater independence, and more say in economic development. It arguably increased women's well-being, too, without dramatically reducing the well-being of men.

Most critically, the shift in working patterns highlighted a major economic anomaly—that a great deal of the unpaid work done in the home, looking after children and the elderly, was actually of considerable value.

Our third proposal is to ensure that all the work done caring for others is properly valued, irrespective of where it takes place.

The best approach to achieve this goal, at least in our opinion, is to organize care work through some sort of formal organization, rather than paying people for working at home alone. Working in an organized way simplifies control, gives the carer a network, and makes it easier to ensure that carers are not exploited. In practice, of course, it would need to be done both ways: formally through organizations and less formally by paying people in the home.

By being paid for the care they provide, those who do this work will be recognized as more socially valuable—in line with those who currently do essentially the same work but in kindergartens and nursing homes. The change would also lead to an increase in GDP, so it would be welcomed by those who see this as a good thing in itself.

Of course, carers would also need to benefit from having a shorter working year, the same as everyone else. Their pay should make proper provision for health insurance and a pension, too.

The simplest way to achieve this change would be for carers to be paid from public budgets so that the total cost is shared by all taxpayers. The problem, of course, is that the majority is unlikely to agree to pay for this—through higher taxes or by directly paying for each hour of care received. Although that may seem an insurmountable hurdle, it is not. Paying carers properly benefits the majority of the population at several points in their lives, whether they are giving care or receiving it. It improves average well-being and helps redistribute income. Many of those being cared for would also benefit, because more motivated people would be looking after them.

The transition from voluntary to paid work would also help soften the impact of aging populations in many rich-world countries. Today, many families find themselves stuck in a situation where they have to care—without pay—for their ailing parents, for years if not decades before they finally are accepted by public or pension fund–supported nursing homes. If this work was properly remunerated, it would reduce the pressure on the public health system, not only by requiring fewer places in nursing homes, but also because it is often cheaper (and better) to care for an elderly person in their home rather than in an institution.

4. INCREASE UNEMPLOYMENT BENEFITS

There will always be some unemployment. There are times when people are between jobs, when seasonal workers cannot find work, and during economic downturns, when businesses lay workers off.

Over the long term, our idea of reducing the length of the working year would reduce the level of unemployment but would not bring it to zero.

Without changes to the welfare systems in much of the developed world, this means that there will still be people without sufficient income. So in a better world, there should be a decent safety net, a welfare system to ensure that those without work can live to much the same standard as those who do have work.

What are the advantages of increasing unemployment benefits?

Paying the unemployed more reduces inequality. It also boosts demand and so protects the jobs and incomes of those in work. And it simplifies the continuous restructuring of the economy, which is necessary to increase productivity, because paying higher welfare benefits makes it (morally) simpler for failing businesses to fire workers. They can then be retrained to work in growing business sectors, knowing that society will pay them decently in the meantime. Finally, higher welfare payments force governments to find the money to pay for the unemployed. It can be done by taxing the rich (who have a lower propensity to consume), borrowing (traditional deficit spending as proposed by Keynes), or printing money and giving it to the unemployed (which amounts to spreading the cost among the whole population, in the form of slightly higher inflation or a lower exchange rate). In all cases, we believe, average well-being will rise.

There are several big advantages to increasing payments to the unemployed. First, and most obviously, it reduces inequality. It also redistributes income, because it forces the government to pay out more to the poor, which encourages them to tax the rich or find alternative socially beneficial sources of income, some of which we will discuss later. It also maintains the incomes of those in work.

How does paying higher unemployment benefits achieve all that?

Increasing welfare payments reduces inequality by increasing the incomes of many of the poorest and most vulnerable people in society. With a higher income, the financial distance between them and those living on an average wage is smaller.

Higher welfare payments also support those in work by making it easier for them to refuse poor rates of pay, turn down jobs that require them to work in unsafe conditions, or accept demands that they work long hours. They make it harder to exploit those with jobs. Better welfare payments tip the balance back in favor of the workers slightly, which is again in the interests of the majority of people.

It is not surprising that high unemployment benefits are resisted by business owners, since they do not typically receive such benefits and have to pay their part of the bill. And it is equally obvious that unemployment benefits must remain below the average wage level so that there remains a positive incentive for workers to find a paying job.

But what is not obvious to many is the positive long-term effect on economic growth of high unemployment benefits. By making it simpler to close down uncompetitive businesses—knowing that workers will still receive a decent income when they are laid off—labor and capital are more easily liberated for new, more productive activities. This phenomenon was illustrated by the rapid economic growth rate of the Nordic countries relative to other rich European economies around the turn of the century and led to the concept of "the Nordic model." [9]

Productivity rises faster—as do average salaries in the long run—because it is simpler to move people from low-productivity to high-productivity jobs when everyone knows they can have a livable income during the transition period.

Of course, higher welfare payments, and so higher wages, will encourage employers to invest in more mechanization and robotization so that they can cut jobs and boost profits. But society can counter this effect through legislation to ensure that the benefit from the productivity rise is distributed fairly and not channeled only to the owners of the robots. This can be achieved through our first proposal—a gradual shortening of the work year—and through some of the other proposals we discuss below.

Higher unemployment benefits also boost demand, because more money will flow through the hands of the less well-off, instead of sitting in the bank accounts of the rich. An increase in demand will spur new investment and so offer a further incentive for enlightened business owners to accept the higher unemployment payments policy. Higher unemployment payments will boost economic growth, in other words.

Of course, our long-term goal for the rich world is to increase average well-being. It is not to increase average incomes and demand but to gradually cut the output and consumption of damaging goods, to reduce emissions, and to slow the pace of resource destruction—all while reducing unemployment and inequality. In order to achieve all of this, the economy needs to be restructured, and this will be resisted unless there is a carrot. There is a need for a short-term advantage that will make restructuring acceptable to the majority. Higher unemployment benefits provide this carrot for the workers. They will not be seen as such by business owners and the rich, of course. But this is not crucial in a democratic society, since the latter two groups are in the political minority.

In the long term, over twenty years perhaps, if working hours per head fall as we propose, average income growth will also slow, as will consumption of materials and energy—that is, the ecological footprint per person. This "green" shift can be accelerated by higher taxes on resources (which we will discuss shortly), which will increase the cost of many goods, and by lower taxes on employment (which we will also discuss). This restructuring of the economy will be simpler and faster if there are higher unemployment payments. Counterintuitively, higher unemployment benefits—and higher material consumption—in the short term will make it simpler to reduce the level of material consumption in the future.

Eventually, higher taxes on resources mean that big businesses will be forced to "rightsize" in the rich world (see Chapter 11 for a discussion of the poor world, which is in a different situation). Dirty business sectors will have to shrink, in other words, to reduce the damaging throughput of raw materials and the consequent emissions of greenhouse gases.

Of course, the rich and big businesses will strongly resist such changes, claiming they are unjust, increase costs, and boost the role of government. Again, though, our ideas should stand a chance of being implemented because they are in the interests of the democratic majority. When most people in the developed world realize that they can work less and still have a decent standard of living, even if they are between jobs, albeit with fewer trinkets, most should understand that this way is better, especially if it gives them some hope that it might also reduce the increasingly frightening weather events that they will be experiencing over the decades ahead.

In our view, the economic system in the rich world will have to shift in this direction anyway, because there is no other (peaceful) alternative. With the prospect of rising unemployment, increasing inequality from mechanization, and the slow emergence of new jobs, following the current path is not in the long-term interests of business owners or the rich either. Without change, there will be fewer jobs, more elderly people, declining populations, and falling demand. Consumption will fall. And that means businesses will suffer, as will banks, because a rising number of people will be unable to pay off their debts. So businesses and the rich should eventually welcome the shift to higher unemployment payments and a more balanced economic system. But it may take time.

Redistribution of wealth, work, and incomes through policies such as higher unemployment benefits and a shorter working year is the best way for businesses and banks to guarantee a stable economic future in the developed world, because it will put more money into the pockets of the poor. It allows the less well-off to spend more, which makes the rate of the economic decay that is going to affect some sectors more manageable, for business, investors, and the banking sector. It makes the economic outlook more predictable for everyone.

The proposal of higher welfare payments (with higher taxes on resources, which the rich and businesses will pay, and lower taxes on employment to encourage businesses to keep staff) meets our criteria, too. Higher unemployment benefits offer immediate gains for the democratic majority, even those in work, and have the added benefit of bringing greater long-term stability to the economy. They increase equality and reduce exploitation.

Higher unemployment payments help to sever the link between jobs and growth. They make it simpler to reduce the output of damaging goods because the closure of dirty carbon-dependent businesses will no longer be seen largely as a threat to jobs but as a first step toward a more climate-friendly economy. People will feel less insecure, knowing that even if they were to lose their current job, it would not bring financial disaster.

To many people, it will seem like we are dreaming. It seems unrealistic to hope that politicians will see the sense in what we are suggesting and introduce long-term policies that meet the needs of the majority. After all, the economic tide today is pushing many rich-world nations in the opposite direction. Governments in many countries want to reduce welfare payments, to "force" people back to work, and to reduce spending in the name of austerity. "The market" will solve the unemployment problem, they say. Individuals need to take responsibility for their welfare themselves.

Business owners support this sort of thinking because it offers them a bigger pool of potential workers to choose from, and the chance to pay people less. But this sort of thinking has been steadily widening the gap between rich and poor, while homelessness has risen and average incomes have fallen. It is not sustainable.

The current approach can go on for only so long. If the developed world is to avoid returning to the social structure that existed in Europe until the twentieth century, where the gap between rich and poor was extremely wide and largely fixed, then something has to change. Inequality has to shrink.

We should mention at this stage that there is an alternative way to raise the money needed to boost welfare payments and reduce inequality without higher business taxes. It is to print money. Governments that control their own currencies could simply print the money needed to give the unemployed a living income without imposing on the private sector at all. If this is done within reason, the consequence would simply be slightly higher inflation, which would spread the costs of higher unemployment benefits across society. The policy would be even more beneficial to social well-being if the unemployed were asked to do useful work while receiving unemployment benefits. We discuss this idea in more detail later.

5. INCREASE TAXATION ON CORPORATIONS AND THE RICH

As we have discussed extensively, one of the big challenges today is widening inequality. If rich nations are to be brought into a less precarious place, there is a need to shift some of the traditional income flowing to the rich over to the poor—that is, to the majority of people who are getting less than their fair share from the current system.

Our first four proposals for a better economic system increase the well-being of the average citizen by boosting basic incomes for everyone (the unemployed, elderly, and unpaid carers) and by sharing the available paid work. In the long run, this is paid for by everyone, through slower consumption growth for those who had a conventional job. In the short run, our proposals can be implemented by businesses paying their staff the same as they do today in return for a shorter working year. But this will not suffice. If the results of our proposals are to survive in the long term, there is a need to increase taxes on businesses and the rich. We will discuss taxes on robots, the dead, and resources shortly.

Is it possible to increase employment by taking from the rich and giving to the poor?

Yes. Under most circumstances, taking from the rich and giving to the poor leads to increased demand in the short term. This is simply because the poor tend to spend all their income—frequently on basics and essentials—whereas the rich save part of what they earn—because they earn more than they need to spend. So shift-ing money from the rich to the poor leads directly to an increase in total demand for consumer goods and services. If you take $1,000 from a rich person, it will simply reduce their savings. If you pass that money to a poor person, they will increase their spending on food, transport, entertainment, clothing, etc., quickly, especially if they believe that the increased money flow will continue. And if the increased money flow looks set to continue, the poor person will increase their regular spending (instead of seeing the payment as a onetime windfall and possibly using it to pay off part of a debt, and so increasing the liquidity of a rich person again).

If a transfer from rich to poor continued, it would result in higher demand for goods and services, which would lead to increased production, which would lead to more jobs and higher wages, which would further stimulate demand. It would lead to increased economic growth, in other words.

Of course, the reduction in the savings of the rich would reduce their assets and so their ability to exploit investment opportunities. In other words, taking from the rich would reduce the number of jobs being created. But this effect is weaker and takes much longer to manifest. In mature economies, with their skewed distribution of wealth, the decision to exploit an invest-ment opportunity is more sensitive to the existence of unmet demand than to the availability of unused collateral.

In practice, the government can ensure a steady transfer from the rich to the poor in two ways. It can increase—on a permanent basis—the taxes taken from the rich and give the money to the poor. Or the government can print money and give it to the poor. In the first case, the total bill is paid for by the rich. In the second case, the bill is paid for by all citizens, who suffer from the (slight) increase in inflation that may occur if the government prints too much money.

Notice, finally, that the proposal to take from the rich and give to the poor works better if there is unemployment at the outset.

In that case, the new demand creates jobs that can be filled by the formerly unemployed without much increase in the general wage level. The best-known example of this was the use of deficit spending to create infrastructure in the United States during the 1930s Depression years.

Of course, a policy of taking from the rich and giving to the poor is normally resisted by the rich. First, they, unsurprisingly, do not like having to pay more. And second, they prefer any newly printed money to flow to them so that they can invest it and earn from the resulting profits. The fact that such investment creates jobs is used by the rich to justify their argument. In reality, even more jobs would have been created—and more quickly, into the bargain—if the same money had been given to the poor.

In recent decades, many large businesses have become adept at evading taxes and, as a consequence, their social responsibilities. Few break the law, but many exploit highly complex legal arrangements, with a variety of holding companies based in obscure places where oversight is limited, to ensure their tax burden is minimized. This is unfair for several reasons. First, it gives these large global companies a competitive advantage, in that they have lower costs than their smaller nationally based rivals, which have to pay taxes. Second, these big companies benefit from the social infrastructure in which they operate—the roads, airports, and rail networks, for example, that are mostly paid for by governments—yet they do not contribute to the cost. This is a particular issue for the finance and banking sector, when it systematically offshores earnings and assets to avoid taxes but bases itself in the main global financial centers, which are rich in infrastructure, and then has to be bailed out by the governments that provide this infrastructure when it runs into trouble.

Paradoxically, at least from a wider social perspective, governments have increasingly supported this sort of tax-avoiding behavior in recent decades. This is because free-market ideologues have told

policy makers that less regulation and more business freedom promotes economic growth, and that "the market" should be allowed
to correct any imbalances. This has resulted in some governments
actively competing with others to lower business taxes in the hope
that big companies will bring investment, jobs, and greater economic
prosperity.

Things have not quite turned out how they anticipated, however.
Rather than landing big investments from big companies and lots of
new jobs, hundreds of unscrupulous companies have simply moved
their headquarters to tax havens or to small countries where their
international business activities will be lightly taxed and regulated.
In addition, they tend to employ only a small number of staff in these
places. They then locate their main business activities in countries
where wages are low, where environmentally damaging activities are
mostly ignored, where it is easier to employ staff as contractors to
avoid social taxes, and where they can deliver goods internationally
and so avoid local sales taxes.

This all makes good business sense, of course, because it boosts
the quarterly returns that are monitored so closely by Wall Street and
rewards business managers. It has even led to businesses playing one
government off against another to get the best deal and to try to persuade them to keep any tax agreements hidden.

None of it makes much sense from a wider social perspective,
however.

As a consequence of these trends, many multinational firms pay
much less tax today than they did thirty-five years ago. Between 1980
and 2010, while the U.S. economy grew by 145%, after-tax business
profits increased by 240%,[10] and they have continued to grow faster
ever since. In 2013, business profits in the United States accounted
for almost 10% of national income, breaking a record set in 1929,
whereas employee compensation was at the lowest level ever with
wages and salaries accounting for barely 40% of the economy.[11]

All this means that businesses and governments, through their
direct support for business, have progressively strengthened the bargaining power of companies, increasing the pressure on societies to

cover the costs of the dispossessed, the unemployed, the elderly, and the environmental damage.

So an important aim of the suggestions we make for a better economic system—and a better world—is to gradually correct this imbalance, by raising the amount of taxes paid by rich individuals and rich corporations.

There are lots of ways this can be achieved, though it may require some degree of international cooperation. If successful, an increase in taxes will gradually change the structure of the economy. There will be a higher demand for public services (those things that governments buy with their increased tax revenue) and a lower demand for investment goods (those things that rich individuals and rich corporations buy with their extra funds). This would lead to higher consumption growth in the short term but lower consumption growth in the long term—because of the lower rate of addition of new capacity. During the transition, there may be a temporary increase in unemployment and smaller business profits, but not in the long run: higher taxes simply change the structure of the economy.

If governments are wise enough to use part of the increased tax income to pay for the production of collective goods such as improved energy efficiency, reduced emissions of greenhouse gases, and a cleaner environment, the tax increase would not only maintain GDP and jobs but also lead to a reduction in the production and consumption of physical goods that increase the human ecological footprint. Taxing businesses properly provides the opportunity to gradually increase the time-horizon of the banking and finance sector, too, reducing the substantial risk it currently presents to economic stability by accentuating and amplifying short-term fluctuations.

Tax revenue from business can be increased in many ways. The simplest way is to increase value-added or corporate income taxes, especially if this is done in a coordinated manner across the rich world, as we have mentioned.

Other methods include the introduction of a financial transaction tax, the removal of certain privileges such as the ability to offset interest payments, levying higher charges on business properties to boost local authority incomes, or ensuring that businesses contribute to infrastructure through road taxes, for example.

Cleverly applied, taxes can even be used to directly reduce the expansion of a nation's ecological footprint. Society can make businesses pay properly for their externalities (we will discuss these later), especially when it comes to carbon and the environment, and even curb their corporate lobbying and advertising activities if these run counter to the interests of the democratic majority. In other words, taxes can be used to gradually change the behavior and attitudes not just of businesses and banks but of society as a whole.

The problem, of course, is getting policy recommendations for higher taxes approved. Although it is true that the majority of people would benefit from higher business taxes—because higher taxes will shift income from the rich to the poor—it is equally true that the majority does not actually welcome higher taxes—even if they are levied on businesses.

This is because many people have been brainwashed into believing that higher business taxes lead to fewer jobs. In fact, higher business taxes shift jobs from the consumption sector—that is, businesses that make consumer goods—to other sectors—public goods and infrastructure, for example. So higher business taxes lower consumption, while maintaining GDP and jobs. The misunderstanding about higher business taxes is, of course, propagated furiously by those who would have to pay them. They spend considerable effort and a great deal of money deliberately trying to confuse the debate, pointing consistently to the negative short-term consequences of higher business taxes.

Higher taxes will be needed not only to bring businesses and banks back into line and cover the cost of higher welfare payments, and so re-balance income inequalities a little. They will also be needed to pay for the costs of climate change, which will rise as the earth gets warmer and the damage spreads. In more general terms, higher taxes will also be needed to help society pay for all those nonprofitable activities needed to create a better world—one of lower unemployment, less inequality, and slower climate change. To make the transition, governments will need a bigger share of the national income.

Another way for them to achieve this is the focus of our next recommendation, the extended use of government-made money—or what we prefer to call green stimulus packages.

6. EXPAND THE USE OF GREEN STIMULUS PACKAGES BY PRINTING MONEY OR RAISING TAXES

We have argued that governments will need more money to increase average well-being in rich societies. They will need this money primarily for spending on collective goods and services—responding to the effects of climate change, improving resource efficiency, protecting biodiversity, and helping the dispossessed, for example. Funding such collective activities through the state is necessary because they do not (yet) provide a good enough return to attract private investors. In other words, extra funds are needed to enable societies to improve well-being according to a plan and not just to restrict themselves to what is profitable in the short term.

Nonprofitable collective activities, like increasing the capacity to generate renewable energy, can be financed through higher taxes—or by printing money. Cranking up the printing presses has the advantage of spreading the cost evenly across society in the form of slightly higher inflation. The idea could also find political support, partly because it would create a number of interesting new jobs in the "cleanup" sector. The "green stimulus packages" adopted by some rich nations after the 2008 financial crisis can serve as a model. At the time, these were even supported by the rich—because they helped boost economic growth (and so businesses' profits).

> **How can stimulus packages increase output and employment?**
>
> Stimulus packages—normally paid for by government debt but also possible through printing money—were famously used in the Great Depression of the 1930s in the United States. The U.S.

government printed new money to pay workers to build infra-structure (roads and national parks, for example). The workers, in turn, went home and spent the money on food, drink, transport, and heating, thereby creating new demand for these goods and services. This higher demand was spotted by businesses, which saw the profit opportunity and built the necessary capacity to sat-isfy the demand.

So distributing money directly to workers in exchange for useful work (ideally outside sectors served by commercial inter-ests) increased the supply of conventional consumer goods and services.

In that particular case, of course, the deficit spending was not large enough to eliminate unemployment. That required the enormous stimulus of the "war effort," with the production of huge amounts of military equipment and jobs in the military for thousands of people. In 1945, three years after the United States entered the war, a full 37% of the U.S. GDP (and jobs, we presume) was accounted for by military output, and little unemployment remained.

This also explains why the stimulus packages after the 2008 financial crisis, known as Quantitative Easing and which we have already discussed, did not work as well as was hoped. The rea-son is that the money was not given to the unemployed but to the rich. And the rich proved unable to find any investment opportu-nities, because there was no unsatisfied demand, so they used the money instead to drive up the cost of other assets (real estate, shares, etc.). Unemployment remained high and GDP growth anemic.

An example of a stimulus package based on printing money is when the People's Congress in China announced in 2014 that it would spend US$800 billion to clean the nation's air and water over the following decade. This will involve paying some 8 million

Chinese engineers and other workers to produce clean air and water, rather than consumer goods and services. These people will receive freshly printed money as wages, which will, of course, be spent on food, housing, and entertainment and so boost domestic demand. So the effort to clean the air will work just like the stimulus packages of the United States during the Depression.

Choosing to increase the average well-being in the long run in China (and the United States) while creating paid jobs in the short term was a political choice. There is, of course, a hidden opportunity cost—which is downplayed—namely the fact that a higher rate of consumption growth would have been achieved if the same money (the same stimulus) was used to pay the same people to produce consumer goods and services.

7. TAX FOSSIL ENERGY AND RETURN THE PROCEEDS IN EQUAL AMOUNTS TO ALL CITIZENS

In 1988, James Hansen, then director of the NASA Goddard Institute of Space Studies and now a professor at Columbia University, was the first scientist to tell a U.S. Senate hearing in persuasive terms that human-made greenhouse gas emissions are an important contributor to global warming and climate change. Since then, he has been on the front line, trying to persuade humanity to change. His central proposal for change in the U.S. is one we strongly support, and in a slightly varied form, it is our seventh proposal for a better world.

Known originally as "tax and dividend," and later as "fee and dividend" because of the unsurmountable opposition against any new taxes in the United States, Hansen's proposal is a simple way to increase the cost of fossil fuels without hurting the poor. He advocates the introduction of a tax on carbon, which would start from a low level and then increase until it is high enough to change the investment behavior, and emissions, of nations. Unlike other taxes, however, 100% of the revenue would be given directly back to citizens—in equal amounts to each of them.

A carbon tax like this would provide every family with a steady income supplement and give everyone a strong incentive to use less fossil energy. It would also increase the competitiveness of nonfossil energy sources, such as solar, wind, and biomass, and so encourage further investment in those sectors. It would promote investment in technologies to reduce CO_2 emissions, too.

Tax and dividend—or "tax and distribute," as we prefer to call it—has obvious redistributive effects. It takes from the rich (who use more energy) and gives to the poor (who use less energy). This should make tax and distribute an acceptable option to the majority of people.

Sadly, Hansen's idea has not been adopted, largely because it would reduce the competitiveness of energy-intensive exports, and because of the deeply ingrained resistance in the United States to any sort of tax. It might stand a better chance of being adopted in other parts of the world, in countries more open to higher taxes—particularly taxes that will contribute to the increased overall well-being of the population and environment—and where the idea of protecting domestic businesses by slapping import duties on foreign energy-intensive products is less alien.

Although the tax would be applied at the source—at the oil well or coal mine—it is easier to explain as follows: Americans consume around 135 billion gallons of gasoline and 46 billion gallons of diesel each year. If each gallon were taxed at one dollar and the proceeds were given to every adult equally, then everyone would get an annual payment of $550. A couple would receive $1,100 a year. This would be paid monthly into their bank account or with a check. All that would be required is a social security number, which would give unregistered immigrants an added incentive to be properly registered. (The payments would not be made to children, as this would encourage population growth.)

Of course, car and sport-utility vehicle (SUV) owners would have to pay more for their fuel, because each gallon of gasoline and diesel would cost a dollar more (this is actually much less than the price has fluctuated in the last decade, so we are sure it would be bearable). On average, everyone would have to spend around $675 more a year on fuel.[12]

So, an average couple with two cars, driving an average mileage, would be worse off. If they had just one car, however, or two cars with European mileage standards (50 miles to the gallon, or more), they would be better off.

Carbon tax and distribute offers a direct incentive for people to drive less and buy cars that offer a higher mileage to the gallon. Families that swapped two SUVs that achieve 18 miles to the gallon for two smaller cars and also drove 25% fewer miles a year would see their net income rise by $850 for little inconvenience. Exhaust emissions would drop dramatically, too.

For the tens of thousands of households in the United States that do not have a car, mostly poorer households, the tax would provide a direct financial windfall.

Taxing coal and natural gas consumption in the same way would boost people's incomes further and provide an additional disincentive for people to burn fossil energy. As already mentioned, the simplest way to do this would be to apply the tax at the point of production, as there are relatively few companies compared to the hundreds of millions of end users. These companies would pass on the tax by charging higher prices to consumers.

So a tax and distribute policy meets our criteria: It should be welcomed by the majority of people, since most will gain. It is the richest, and those who waste the most energy and produce the most emissions, who will not like our proposal. But they will have an incentive to change their ways and could even be offered time and support to make the transition.

There is one additional benefit. A one dollar carbon tax per gallon of fuel is not only high enough to modify the behavior of energy consumers, but also high enough to influence the behavior of investors because, since it amounts to around one hundred dollars per ton of CO_2, it makes many actions that reduce climate gas emissions profitable.[13]

It also provides an incentive to switch to renewable energy sources and encourages consumers to buy more energy-efficient appliances and manufacturers to make them. Architects and real

estate developers would see demand rise for energy-efficient buildings. And it would discourage people from leaving the lights on when
they do not need them, as well as building civic awareness of energy
being used inefficiently. Pressure would grow for the lights that burn
in shop windows at 3:00 a.m. to be switched off. Car makers would
have a strong incentive to build cars with lower fuel consumption,
too, which they can easily do in the United States without much
investment. Many European cars—even those made in the EU by
U.S. companies—can achieve 70 miles to the gallon, more than three
times the average in the U.S. today.

It is not just fuel and energy prices that would rise as a result of
carbon taxes like these, of course. The cost of food and many other
goods would increase, depending on the amount of fossil fuel energy
needed to produce and deliver them. This increase would be offset
by other advantages: it would boost sales of local produce and cut
imports of fruit and vegetables from distant places (assuming they
were taxed on their carbon footprint, too).

As the economy became more energy efficient, the dividend
being paid to each individual would obviously begin to fall. There
are two ways around this. First, the rate of tax can rise steadily, maintaining the incentive to improve energy efficiency and reduce fossil
fuel use, or governments could tax something else in a similar way.
Or they could do both.

The principle of taxing something that damages society in the
long term—to make it more expensive and reduce its use—and distribute the resulting income to all adult citizens in equal amounts—so
that they can buy at least some more of the forbidden fruit, or more
wisely use the money to buy something else that satisfies their
desires in more societally beneficial ways—can be applied to things
other than fossil fuels, too. It could be applied to road pricing, for
example, where people would pay more to drive privately owned cars
in the rush hour, with the revenue paid out to everyone, so subsidiz-
ing those who only use public transport. This would be especially
easy to implement in cities where congestion charging already exists,
but where the local authorities currently retain the revenues.

So the tax and redistribute policy meets our criteria. It benefits the majority immediately and helps reduce emissions, which helps the planet.

8. SHIFT TAXES FROM EMPLOYMENT TO EMISSIONS AND RESOURCE USE

Just as many people cannot readily grasp that something is "infinite," when it has no beginning, middle, or end, many appear to have the same problem with the word "finite." There is an oft-repeated quote by Kenneth Boulding, John F. Kennedy's environmental advisor, who said, "Anyone who believes in indefinite growth in anything physical, on a physically finite planet, is either mad or an economist." It contains two words that are frequently forgotten when the comment is repeated, however: "physical" and "physically."

This is important, because humanity *can* have infinite economic growth if it wishes. What it cannot have is infinite economic growth that requires a never-ending increase in the use of Earth's physical resources, because these are limited, they are finite. Nor is it possible to have endless economic growth that releases ever-increasing amounts of greenhouse gases into the planet's atmosphere.

As Boulding also pointed out, humanity actually lives on a gigantic and very isolated spaceship—that is, Earth—and nothing is going to increase the natural resources available to any measurable degree in any time frame with which humanity is currently familiar. So there is a need to manage the use of raw materials carefully, as many are limited.

Humanity can have as much economic growth as it wants, however, because GDP is measured by value, not quantity. If people increase the value of what they do, after taking account of inflation, GDP will rise.

That does not mean society does not need to change, however. As well as promoting sustainable sorts of economic growth, humanity needs to reduce its resource use and emissions from their currently unsustainable levels. Society needs the sort of growth that reduces the human ecological footprint, that leads to a decline in humanity's use of scarce resources, that cuts emissions and pollution, and that stops biodiversity destruction. It needs "green growth."

What is green growth?

In this book we use the strictest definition of "green growth."

Green growth is an increase in GDP that goes along with a reduction in the ecological footprint (EF). Green growth can come from a new activity (e.g., building and running a sewerage plant) that leads to reduced emissions. Or it can result from replacing two small and dirty factories (e.g., paper mills) with a single larger and cleaner one. The marginal case is when one dirty activity (e.g., producing fifty thousand polluting cars a year at $40,000 a car) is replaced with an activity that has exactly the same GDP—the same value added per year but that reduces the EF—(e.g., producing forty thousand clean cars a year at $50,000 a car).

In this case, the change in GDP—which we call ΔGDP—is zero. But the shift from dirty to clean cars leads to a decline in the footprint, so ΔEF < 0.

In summary, by green growth, we mean ΔGDP $\geq$ 0 and ΔEF < 0.

Other people use softer definitions. They regard an increase in GDP as "green" even if ΔEF = 0 (like when a hairdresser cuts hair more often). Some even go so far as to call it green growth when ΔGDP/ΔEF of the new project is bigger than ΔGDP/ΔEF in the traditional approach. An example is when a nation decides to build a new gas-powered plant instead of a new coal-fired plant. The gas project has a third of the greenhouse gas emissions per kWh compared to the coal-based plant. We do not support the idea that this is "green," however, because it does not reduce the ecological footprint, only the rate of growth in the footprint.

We want to make sure that "green growth" leads to ever-lower use of resources each year and not only to "decoupling" (which is lower growth in resource use than in GDP). But we are fully aware that others apply different definitions.

What does it mean to run out of resources?[14]

When natural resources (such as oil or gold) are "used up," it means that they become increasingly difficult to get hold of. They are deeper down, in poorer grades, situated in less friendly territory, or available only through recycling. They then become more expensive, because it takes more labor and capital to maintain the traditional flow of resources (measured in tons per year). This labor and capital is then no longer available to produce consumer goods and services. So the macro-level effect of "running out of resources" is a forced reduction in the consumption of other goods and services. The effect—the reduction in consumption—will be smaller if substitutes for the resource in question appear more quickly.

With green growth, it is possible to reduce humanity's damaging impact on the planet to a sustainable level and still have healthy, vibrant, and, if desired, growing economies. Societies just need to stop promoting the sort of economic growth that requires the use of ever more of Earth's valuable nonrenewable resources.

Economic growth can also be achieved by improving resource efficiency—that is, the amount of value created from every ton of resources used. In many industrial sectors today, raw materials and energy are used extremely inefficiently, partly because they are far too cheap and largely because of something economists refer to as externalities.

An externality is a consequence of an activity that is either unforeseen or deliberately ignored. A negative externality of burning fossil fuels, for example, is that chemicals and particles enter the air. These cause respiratory problems, as well as other health difficulties, make urban life gray and dreary, and are one of the main causes of climate change. But current practice is for businesses to ignore these costs when they calculate the prices they charge and their profitability.

They are generally ignored by economists, too, who do not include them when they calculate GDP.

This is plainly misguided from a long-term social perspective, because the costs of these externalities can be extremely high and are often not very hard to quantify. Society knows what it costs to treat respiratory problems and can put a value on the lives shortened by smog. It is also possible to work out what climate change has cost so far and to make estimates about the future costs.

Fortunately, there has been progress in tracking externalities in the last forty years. Economists, and others, now use something called "cost-benefit analysis" to estimate the unintended and uncounted effects of business and other human activities in monetary terms.

We propose that this development be taken to the next stage, and that these costs should not just be estimated but charged back to businesses and governments in exchange for the right to use resources and create emissions. This would not stop the negative externalities in the short term, of course. But it would create an incentive for businesses and society to reduce or stop their damaging behavior in the long run.

This is necessary because externalities are not obscure and isolated economic considerations. They are everywhere, and they are usually extremely undesirable.

The price paid for carbon-based fuel ignores not only the environmental damage caused when it is burned, for example, but also the environmental damage caused during its extraction. Nor does the price of a barrel of oil, bag of coal, or therm of gas take into account the steady depletion of these resources, or the implications of this for future generations. Classical economics says it should.

It is externalities that allow companies to sell many foodstuffs more cheaply than they should, because they do not pay the full costs of the fuels needed to produce them. Nor do they pay for the environmental damage caused by artificial fertilizers that pollute rivers or for the consequences of the hormones that are pumped into animals and often make them ill.

Just as lung cancer was for many years an externality of smoking cigarettes, ignored by the producers, many of today's fastest-growing health problems are (often well-known) externalities of food manufacturers putting too much sugar, fat, and salt into what they produce. The obesity, unhappiness, and shortened lives that result are paid for by society, not by the businesses that cause them.

Because today's economic thinking means that businesses are rewarded for rising quarterly returns, it is in their interests to outsource as many externalities as possible and ignore (and often deny) any long-term negative social consequences of their actions.

To properly account for these externality costs, we propose that societies should charge them back through what are known as Pigovian taxes. These correct market failures, which is what externalities really are, by charging the full costs back to producers (who will, of course, pass them on to the consumers, who will hopefully react to the higher prices by choosing less damaging products).

Pigovian taxes have many benefits. Businesses pay properly for the consequences of their actions, and governments gain a source of revenue to cover some of the costs incurred (for healthcare and fighting pollution, for example). Rather than the costs of damaging business activities being "socialized"—that is, carried unwittingly by society, the environment, and future generations—as they are now, they are charged back to those incurring them.

Pigovian taxes give businesses a powerful reason to reduce many of the damaging things they do, to take full responsibility for their activities, and to become much more efficient. And they make everyone more aware of the problems caused by these businesses, which is an additional advantage.

To make sure this becomes a virtuous cycle, governments can ratchet up the tax rates applied as businesses become more efficient so that there is a continuous incentive for them to innovate, to use fewer of the world's scarce resources, and to create less pollution.

Of course, a consequence of Pigovian taxes is that the price paid for almost everything will rise—in some cases substantially. Fossil energy in particular will become more expensive. So these new taxes will probably need to be applied gradually, to give everyone time to adjust.

Such taxes can greatly reduce the human ecological footprint—but only if governments do not spend the resulting revenues on activities that are even more damaging, and consumers do not respond by increasing their ecological footprint in other ways. This is known as the rebound effect.

The rebound effect explains why it is always essential to ask where money that is not used on one thing (so reducing one type of damaging footprint) is being used instead (potentially increasing another sort of damaging footprint). For example, when someone insulates their home they use less fossil fuel energy and this reduces climate gas emissions. But if the house owner uses the money saved on fuel to fly to Paris or New York for a weekend's shopping, the climate gas emissions from that single trip could be higher than all the savings made by installing the insulation.

So, paradoxically, increasing the tax on electricity can lead to higher emissions in the long run. The only solution to this problem is for society to increase the tax on all the uses of a resource it wants to limit the use of. This is the basis for the dream about a global tax on resources (modeled after the elusive global carbon price). Of course, such a global tax is unlikely ever to be adopted, but that does not mean governments should abandon the idea of taxing resources and externalities properly.

Pigovian and other resource and emissions taxes can be used to gradually shift economies' reliance on damaging activities—those that use lots of nonrenewable natural resources, sidestep social responsibilities, create lots of pollution, or destroy ecosystems—toward activities that are not as dependent on scarce raw materials, are socially beneficial, and do not damage the environment. They help society replace damaging economic activities with less harmful ones.

It is also very important to remember that this work will never end. There will always be externalities that should have been paid for and that need to be identified and taxed.

This is not to say that humanity should put a price on everything, of course, or assume that because something has a value it should be viewed in purely economic terms.

Society should not put a price on tigers, the sky, rain, or love, for example, because such items cannot be valued in simple monetary terms. To do so is dangerous, even, because it encourages some people to think that these things can be traded, bought, and sold. Society should only put a price on the externalities that apply to the goods and services that are bought and sold, to correct market failings, and should seek another mechanism to protect everything else that is desirable.

So society will need to think about how to apply these taxes very carefully. But just because applying them is complicated does not mean it should not be done.

Although higher raw materials and externality cost taxes would greatly increase business costs, the revenues would allow governments to tax labor less and so reduce the cost to businesses of employing people. That trade-off could go some way toward winning a modicum of acceptance from the business world for our proposal.

The proceeds from resource and externality taxes could also be used to reduce the sales (or value-added) tax on goods and services that improve average well-being. Governments could reduce taxes on healthy foods, medical care, education, and some recreational activities, for example, to encourage people to live healthier, more fulfilling, and ultimately happier lives. This would help provide support for change, too.

Governments might even subsidize some of these items, rather than fossil fuels, as many do now. (We acknowledge, of course, that many of the much-criticized subsidy systems for fossil fuels are among the only working transfers of income to the poor. The problem is these transfers are usually done in ways that benefit big energy users even more. What is needed is to limit any subsidy to a reasonable annual use—for example, to the first 50 gallons of fuel used per person per year. Modern information technology would make such a rationing scheme simple, even in large populations.)

Some people will argue that governments promoting healthier lifestyles in this way is a step too far toward the "nanny state," claiming that people should have the freedom to choose what they eat and do themselves, without any nudging or herding tactics from regulators. They will say that businesses should be free from any unnecessary costs and social burdens—the current mantra of extreme free-market ideology.

But, we would argue, if this comes at the cost of excess use of scarce resources, exploding healthcare budgets, and accelerating climate change, there is more than a moral duty for the state to intervene. It has a social responsibility. Besides, nannies are not such a bad thing: their role is to help and guide those in their care to grow and develop into responsible adults. They generally have a positive influence, just as taxation and government should have on society.

9. INCREASE DEATH TAXES

"There is no point more difficult to account for than the right we conceive men to have to dispose of their goods after death."
ADAM SMITH

The aim of our ninth proposal is to reduce inequality. Increasing estate duties—transferring most of a person's wealth to society upon their death—has many effects, but the main one we are interested in is its potential to narrow differences in income and wealth. It will also reduce philanthropy, and we believe that this would be wise, too.

There are two ways to interpret the common expression "there are no pockets in a shroud." One is to see it as an endorsement of the good life. People should spend every last cent before they die and use their money to enjoy their lives. The other is simply to recognize that people cannot take their material assets with them when they die.

In some cultures, people's possessions are burned with their corpse. In the rich world, they are traditionally passed on to children or other relatives. This is very nice for those who receive these windfalls. If you happen to be born to parents who are wealthy enough to leave you something, or you befriend someone who decides to pass on their accumulated possessions when they die, you gain financially without doing any economically valuable work (we would exclude most carers here). For most people who receive an inheritance, there is not much effort required.

For the majority of people in the world, who inherit nothing, this situation is patently unfair. Most people do not have a chance to win the legacy lottery, because they are unable to play.

For those who can, though, the gains can be life changing. Discovering that you are suddenly thousands, or tens of thousands, or even millions of dollars richer almost overnight allows some people to transform their lives in ways that the majority can only dream of. They can invest in their own education, buy a home, or take a cruise. Some can even retire on the proceeds and live a life of leisure. Many schools and other academic institutions, as well as many hospitals and children's homes, currently benefit in similar ways that have little economic or social logic. Rather, the donations of the dead can strengthen their reputations and positions, not necessarily because of what they have achieved for society, but simply because they have greater financial clout.

As most inheritance laws are currently formulated, a small percentage of the population is able to gain, and the gains can accumulate from one generation to another, whereas the majority of people live in a *Groundhog Day*-like financial cycle, where each generation starts with the same low level of wealth as the last and never manages to progress beyond that. A small percentage of people have an opportunity to live better lives because of the randomness of their birth, in other words, not through their own efforts. The wealthy deceased knowingly commit one of Mahatma Gandhi's seven deadly sins by providing "wealth without work" to a small share of the population.

It is also well known that providing the poorest people in society with a basic income, be they in the rich world or the poor world, transforms lives. It improves education standards and medical care, as well as diets and quality of living.[15]

So there is an injustice on one side and a need on the other, which can neatly cancel each other out if society chooses.

Free-market thinking on inheritance is greatly outdated, partly because it is the result of ideas that were developed during the European Enlightenment. Much is the result of the thinking of seventeenth-century philosopher John Locke, who argued that everyone has a right to life, liberty, and property. It is the word "property" that concerns us here, for it has led to many current ideas about death and economics that should be changed, because they are no longer appropriate in modern societies. Locke argued, for example, that Earth should be considered the property of people, that it exists for humanity's survival and benefit. This, as well as much religious thinking, is what leads many to believe that they can plunder and pollute the planet without conscience, even today, because they have been told—and have never stopped to question—that nature is there for humanity's use.

When it comes to property, in the sense of goods and chattels, Locke started with the premise that we each own our bodies. It is, therefore, logical, he argued, that we also own anything that is the result of work done by those bodies. When labor, which is logically our own property, he argued, is added to an outside object, then that too becomes ours. He said that when we pick an apple from a tree it becomes our property, because we did work to get it. He argued, too, that we can gain ownership of land by working it, as long as it is not owned by someone else.

Locke (and many others) argued that individuals enter into a contract with society in order to protect their property, partly because their property becomes part of who they are. But he also argued strongly that people always need to leave enough land for others, to ensure that through property ownership no one is worse off than they were before. Like almost all Enlightenment thinkers, he had strong moral principles behind his proposals, and he believed strongly that people are equal. The goal of many Enlightenment philosophers was to improve average living standards and lift people out of poverty, not provide a mechanism for social division.[16] Adam Smith's writings on the economy take the same approach; he believed strongly in humans' innate sociability, in their desire to work together for the good of others and society.

This thinking, and subsequent developments, has had many positive consequences for hundreds of millions of people over several centuries but has also created some economic and social oddities. The idea that individual property rights are seen to come from nature or God, for example, is very difficult to defend today, yet it still lies behind the idea that the planet is there for humanity to exploit. Similarly, some property rights, especially those for intellectual property, sometimes take precedence over human rights, leading to injustices. When these concern access to medication, for example, they can even lead to tragedy. Today's notions about property also encourage society to think it is reasonable for companies and individuals to own the world's resources, including water, for financial gain. Legally, this means that some individuals have the right to deliberately destroy the world's natural resources, should they so wish, without having to answer to others, or to broader society.

Historical ideas about property have also led to the current belief that "what is mine becomes yours when I die," despite there being no "market" for the transfer and the recipient rarely doing anything economically useful to earn their windfall. It perpetuates inequality, not just of income but also of opportunity. Those who inherit wealth have an advantage over those who do not, because it is easier to make progress when you are already rich.

So our ninth proposal to reinvent prosperity and create a better world is to gradually remove this unfair transfer of wealth and for governments to review property laws to remove many of the other injustices. This goes hand in hand with the emerging view in the major religions that humanity's role is that of steward of the planet, not of owner.

We suggest that death duties should be progressive and rise, perhaps even to 100%, so that everyone begins life with the same chance of winning. Of course, the details need to be thought through carefully, so that financial gifts by the living are taxed, too, and the needs of partners remaining after the death of their spouse or partner are considered.

We are not the first to propose high death duties, of course. Ironically, many of the richest people in the world support them, too. Like Theodore Roosevelt and Thomas Paine, Adam Smith believed in hefty estate taxes: "A power to dispose of estates forever is manifestly absurd. The Earth and the fullness of it belongs to every generation, and the preceding generation can have no right to bind it up for posterity. Such extension of property is quite unnatural."[17]

Such a change in taxation would, of course, encourage some people to spend everything before they die. But there are limits to what people can spend, and many people just like to hoard what they have. So we believe that the vast majority of those in a position to offer an inheritance would die just as rich as they do today. The main difference would be that instead of the money being bequeathed to their children, or to a cause of their choice, it would end up with the state, where it could be used for the betterment of wider society instead.

Although there may be many side effects of an inheritance tax, none of them appears likely to undermine its prime goals, which are to ensure that fewer people start their lives financially far ahead of others and that society gets to decide which activities are worthwhile, not the rich.

Again, requiring a transfer of most of the wealth of an individual to the state upon death meets our criteria, in that it offers an immediate advantage for the democratic majority.

High estate taxes would severely damage the world of philanthropy, of course, and at first glance this would appear to be a bad thing.

Charities and philanthropic foundations are generally seen as being beneficial to society because they support so many causes deemed to be "good" or "worthy." Yet the very existence of such organizations means that parts of the economic system are not working properly. If children are dying from malnutrition, species are being killed off, or companies are damaging the environment, there is a big underlying problem that is not being properly addressed.

What charitable institutions and philanthropists are doing is mopping up the problems they find bothersome—rather than leaving them, like a puddle, for all to see. They become substitutes for healthy social responsibility because they postpone the reorganization of society into one where such negative externalities do not exist in the first place.

Charities and philanthropic organizations also depend on the desires of their unaccountable donors. It is the managers of these organizations who decide where and how money should be spent, and which causes they choose to support. As a consequence, their donations are frequently subject to favoritism, waste, and inefficiency. Just as it is easier for a zoo to get visitors to sponsor the tigers, leaving the vast majority of the other animals unsupported, philanthropy supports society's tigers. The rich give to causes that appeal to them, or where they may have a personal agenda, rather than to causes where there is the greatest need. They frequently impose conditions on their giving, too—to discourage the use of contraceptives, or to promote their country's values or some religion, for example. Although governments are subject to public scrutiny, the philanthropy business is not.

Moreover, philanthropists rarely fight for social justice. Quite the opposite. Their actions are typically founded on an acceptance of injustice, partly because they are its byproduct. It may be laudable for philanthropists to try to improve people's lives by offering medicines, encouraging research, financing schools, or bringing water to the poor. But most of this money promotes Western ideas of progress and development—often explicitly so. It allows wealthy individuals and their philanthropic organizations to play God and decide what is worthy—without being answerable to society for what they do. Genuine need should not be dependent on handouts at the whim of the rich.

Increasing death taxes would help remove this unwelcome social anomaly.

10. ENCOURAGE UNIONIZATION

One of the most important ways to achieve a better balance in societies between those who own businesses and those who do most of the work—and so create most of the value—is to encourage unionization. Only by working together can the majority exert any real influence over their legitimate claim for a fair share of the economic value that they help to create.

Unionization is essential in the battle against inequality and exploitation, and we find it sad that many rich-world societies no longer seem to understand its importance in defending the interests of the majority and so have allowed the role of unions to decline. When times were good and wages rose "by themselves," this made some sense. But they are no longer rising in much of the rich world, where, as we have discussed, the living standards of millions are stagnating or falling. This leads us to believe that there will be renewed interest in people acting together. We want to encourage this.

Many people do not understand that the primary role of a modern union is not to squeeze more income from the bosses, though the pursuit of fairness is still of great importance. Its most important role in postindustrial service economies is to put pressure on politicians. Unions encourage those in power to play a more constructive role in the creation of a better society—one that works to improve the well-being of the average citizen.

This is especially important because many of today's elected representatives are not doing their jobs as they should. They are failing to address immigration problems in Europe and the United States, failing to stop wars and conflict, failing to reduce inequality and unemployment, and failing to respond to climate change in any useful way. This may be partly understandable, given the short time-horizon of most voters and the market. Still, it is undesirable, and it opens an opportunity for unions to play a larger role again, to encourage politicians to think more about the long-term needs of society. But for this to happen, they need to become stronger.

Although it might be difficult for those under the age of fifty living in the English-speaking world to believe, unions were long viewed as essential by the majority of people in the rich world. They represented the side of the workers in the seemingly eternal fight between those who own businesses, and want to maximize their profits, and those who work in them, and want to be treated fairly. Through collective action, unions were seen as protectors of the workers, and they achieved better pay and conditions for millions of people throughout much of the twentieth century. They played a vital role in reducing inequality, too.

In recent decades, though, many people, including many of those who traditionally benefited from collective action, have come to see unions as largely unnecessary, especially in the Anglo-Saxon world. This view has been greatly encouraged by employers, free-market ideologues, and many modern-day economists.

As a 2015 International Monetary Fund (IMF) study[18] points out, however, the declining rate of unionization has had direct consequences on incomes and inequality. It notes that over the last thirty years in many countries, wages have stagnated or fallen, unemployment has risen, and inequalities have widened. The study points out that strong unions encourage income and wealth redistribution, as well as stronger social and labor rights, by encouraging workers to vote for parties that promote greater fairness—and vice versa. It finds that weak unions result in greater inequalities and weaker social rights.

Because de-unionization reduces the bargaining power and incomes of employees, it increases the incomes of the top managers and shareholders. Productivity gains are paid to the rich, rather than being spread more evenly among those who create them. Weaker unions also reduce the influence of employees when it comes to corporate decisions, such as factory closures and executive compensation. The IMF study also points out that less powerful unions are associated with reductions in the minimum wage, which "increases inequality considerably."[19]

So our next proposal is a nudge to action, a call to arms, as it were. It is to encourage those with jobs, and even those without jobs, to participate in unions, to strengthen the collective voice.

This will have direct and immediate benefits, as long as enough people get involved. A study by the Economic Policy Institute[20] shows that unionized workers earn around a quarter more than nonunionized workers. Unions are particularly valuable to low- and middle-income workers, especially those without a college degree. In the United States, union members are more likely to receive paid leave,[21] health insurance,[22] and employer-provided pensions.[23] They are also more likely to receive better pensions and substantially longer paid vacation time. Unions are also found to play a vital role in improving worker safety, ensuring overtime pay, and ensuring workers are entitled to family leave and medical leave.

Most critically, unions are vital to ensure the smooth restructuring that is necessary in any economy. If there is to be economic growth, unprofitable companies have to be replaced by others that can create more value per hour of work. Modern unions understand that such restructuring is unavoidable, and that it is counterproductive to insist on the continuation of unprofitable activities (as long as this lack of profitability is not because of excessive management pay, financial trickery, or very high dividends for business owners).

Modern unions seek to ensure that workers are protected during the transition between jobs, that society provides people with an income, and that workers are retrained for their next job when necessary. Powerful unions, ideally representing more than 50% of the workforce, are able to put in place the mechanisms that simplify the process of improving business efficiency. In much of northern Europe, and notably in Germany, unionization remains high. Yet productivity growth is also high, and unemployment remains low. Unions and employers work in cooperation, not competition or conflict, supported by local and national regulations that encourage this.[24]

Studies consistently show that unions play an important role in oiling the wheels of good society, in making the machine run smoothly. This is not how they are portrayed in much of the media or by right-leaning politicians and business leaders who downplay the long-term social benefits of powerful modern unionization, of course. They oppose unions because unions shift economic power from business owners to workers in the short term.

Yet studies show that unionization also helps to promote social and intergenerational mobility, because children born to low-income families typically go on to earn higher incomes if their parents were union members.[25] Perhaps this is because being part of a union encourages people to think about individual rights and social advancement in a fundamental way.

Much of the decline in unionization over the last thirty years has been the result of social, economic, and political changes that are the direct consequence of an economic model that seeks to free business from regulatory influences, from paying for negative externalities, or from accepting many social responsibilities. This extreme free-market ideology makes sense for shareholders, because it makes them richer in the short term. But it is a lose-lose game in the long term, because it slows the rate of economic growth that could have been achieved through cooperation. If the influence of business is pushed too far, as happened when extreme austerity measures were imposed on Greece after the 2008 financial crisis, it eventually reduces demand by cutting off the fuel to the consumption-driven economic engine.

The trend to outsource business activities to contractors has weakened the influence of many unions recently, too, with workers finding it harder to mobilize collective bargaining power. Reversing this trend will be difficult, though not impossible. Contractors and the self-employed should fight for legislative support to ensure they have the same legal protection and rights as employees. Their first step should be to join a union, to strengthen its effort to promote change. A second step would be to ensure that the unions work to promote not only the interests of those who have jobs but also the interests of those who do not by, for example, improving unemployment benefits and other welfare payments.

11. RESTRICT TRADE

The notion of free trade has evolved over the last half century to the point where it is almost sacrosanct, because it is generally believed that openness to trade benefits everyone. This is no longer true, however. Regulations that promote free trade were generally beneficial when societies were poor and there was a need to increase total output. But this is no longer the case in the rich world, where the main objective is not to produce more socks and furniture but to create more jobs. If unemployment is a major problem, more liberalized trade can actually make the situation worse, because it makes it easier for businesses to move abroad, reducing domestic employment.

We believe that it is time for the rich world to rethink the regulation of trade. As people have become used to an ever-more open world, our proposal might appear heretical to many. We freely admit that it is a major break with current policy. What we are proposing would also require time and effort to implement, because it would involve dismantling, softening, and perhaps even violating hard-fought trade agreements. Yet constraining free trade can be good, especially when the goal is to protect jobs, reduce inequality, and slow climate change.

Originally, economists such as Adam Smith encouraged free trade because it allowed countries to specialize, to focus on industries and businesses where they had a competitive advantage, and to trade with countries that had different advantages. A country with ample reserves of coal but no sheep could trade with one that had no coal but lots of sheep, and both would be better off. Such specialization allowed countries to invest in their most advantageous industries and business sectors, to develop economies of scale and lower their costs, while creating new jobs and developing defensible skills. It lowered unit costs, which expanded markets and so was mutually beneficial for trading societies.

Today, open borders and free trade frequently mean something different. Today, free trade is—first and foremost—the mechanism that allows companies to move their factories to countries with lower labor costs to boost their profits. In the process, they destroy domestic jobs and leave wider society to pick up the costs of the resulting unemployment and social deprivation.

Free trade agreements not only allow companies to do this, but actually force them to do it to remain competitive. Because they are able to import whatever they produce overseas without restriction, their goods are cheaper. So a steel company can shut a plant in northern England and supply English customers at a lower cost from a new factory (possibly using the same equipment) located in China. Jobs are lost in England, and although they are gained in China, the workers in China receive a lower rate of pay. From the perspective of the workers, it is not a zero-sum game. The workers in England lose more than those in China gain.

Nor is it a zero-sum game for business: profits increase, as do dividends to shareholders. As these profits typically flow back to the rich world, boosting the incomes of the wealthy, inequality there rises. Thanks to open markets, in other words, income is transferred from workers to business owners. This is why businesses fight so feverishly to support free trade arrangements.

New free trade rules, currently in the legislative pipeline,[26] will even make it possible for businesses to sue governments if they "diminish their expected future profits"[27]—putting the rights of companies above those of employees and wider society. They will also reduce environmental protection standards to lower production costs and, by changing patent legislation, make access to many medicines much more complex and expensive, all in the name of boosting short-term profits.

There would, of course, be consequences if trade were to be constrained. The price of many goods would rise, and so consumption would decrease. But that would be good for the environment, especially if any new tariffs led to a decline in the sale of carbon-intensive products, such as cheap plastic toys made using coal-derived power in Asia. Similarly, if trade regulations meant that fewer goods were shipped around the world, less fuel would be needed and so carbon emissions would decline.

So trade restrictions can help slow the pace of climate change, too.

In response to this proposal, many economists and businesspeople argue that if companies are protected by trade barriers, they will be shielded from the beneficial effects of international competition. They will become fat and inefficient and cease to invest or innovate.

This is, however, something of a spurious argument. It assumes that domestic firms are not subject to local competition and that higher consumption of everything is good. Although boosting consumption and output were once useful objectives, that is not the case in the rich world today, when the main social challenges are unemployment, inequality, and climate change.

It is true, however, that increasing tariffs in one country (say, Britain) will slow job creation in another country (say, China). But this would force China to focus on developing its domestic economy, rather than relying on export-led growth. It may be good and noble for rich countries to help poor countries develop, but if it leads to higher unemployment, greater inequality, and unsustainable social friction, the policy is not sustainable.

Trade barriers can also be used—actually, they will have to be used—by any nation that wants to deviate from the philosophy of the cheapest solution (the lowest-cost way to produce something) and still participate in global trade. If a country wants to protect nature more than its trading partners, it will logically have to shy away from products that contribute to the planet's destruction.

The only way to do this in a world of profit-maximizing firms is to protect responsible producers through imposing tariffs on irresponsible producers—or banning those producers altogether. The same argument applies to any nation that wants to reduce its consumption of products that emit greenhouse gases, or that rely on child labor or on people working very long hours, for example.

By imposing tariffs on undesirable, but cheap, products, a progressive nation encourages politicians in less progressive nations to shift in the right direction, too—toward an economic system with fewer negative externalities and fairer employment conditions.

In proposing greater protectionism, we need to emphasize that we are not looking backward to an era of closed markets and isolationism but forward to a time when trade is balanced and managed in the interests of society and humanity's ecological footprint. We are arguing for healthy trade policies to allow rich-world economies to make the structural changes they need to shift to a more sustainable and balanced economic system. Protectionism will reduce the risks facing employees during the transition, making it possible for people to maintain higher levels of well-being.

Higher tariffs can also generate an income for governments to boost welfare spending and fight the effects of climate change. Used properly, higher trade barriers can be a win-win option, paid for by reduced consumption growth but leading to less unemployment, lower inequality, and slower global warming.

12. ENCOURAGE SMALLER FAMILIES

There is one especially unconventional—and potentially controversial—policy that we wish to propose. It is to reward those families who have one child only, or none.

For humanity to bring its ecological footprint below the carrying capacity of the planet, there are two options: reduce the population or reduce the footprint per person. Since the latter is extremely difficult, and often seen as an attack on well-being, the first—reducing the population, or number of potential consumers—emerges as an interesting option. A practical way of doing this would be to encourage smaller families in the rich world—and by smaller, we mean one child or none at all.

The subject of population control is sensitive—no one likes to be told by their government that they cannot have children. It is seen as a basic human right for those who are able.

However, it is also an incontrovertible fact that the doubling of the population in the last fifty years has been the biggest cause of the increase in humanity's ecological footprint. Technological developments have actually kept the footprint per person more or less constant, but because the population has doubled, so has the total footprint.

Common sense says that this growth in the number of human beings and their ecological footprint cannot go on forever. Thankfully, improvements in education, health, and contraception mean that the average number of children per woman in the world has already fallen.[28] This is not enough, however. To secure a better future, it would help greatly if society slowed the rate of population growth even more, and ideally even made it negative.

There are few historical examples of nations choosing to limit their populations. Until the 1800s, kings, queens, emperors, and the Church mostly wanted populations to grow. They wanted as large a population as possible to extend their wealth and power. It was the presence of people that allowed those in charge to convert nature's bounty into something of use for the elite. So those in charge encouraged their subjects, or followers, to procreate. Even then, it took a very long time to populate the planet, mainly because of the regular appearance of famines and pestilences, but also because of wars, as those same leaders sought to extend their wealth and power even more.

In more recent times, a number of countries have tried to manage their populations, notably China. In the late 1970s, China instituted the one-child policy for most of the population, with hefty punishments for those who evaded the law. Although this policy remains highly controversial, and it has had some unwelcome social and economic side effects, it remains one of the best examples ever of one generation making a sacrifice for the benefit of future generations. But it has also led to more selfishness, higher divorce rates, and a less cohesive society—a generation of what are known locally as "little emperors" and "little empresses" who, having been doted on as single children, find it extremely hard to form lasting relationships.

This policy was gradually relaxed over the years, and finally became a two-child policy in 2016, though by that time the Chinese population had stabilized at around 1.3 billion people, at least 400 million fewer than it would otherwise have been. This has greatly reduced China's current and future ecological footprint, by cutting the demand for resources and energy. China may have horrendous pollution problems, and huge resource challenges, but they are much smaller than once expected.

In much of the rich world, population growth has slowed in the last thirty years, too, though for other reasons. The average number of children per woman in the EU15 countries fell below 2.1 as long ago as 1970. This is the magical threshold, the number needed to maintain a stable population in the long run, without any growth. Since then, it has fallen even further, to nearer 1.3. As a consequence, many European nations face shrinking workforces. Some have tried to boost birth rates again by offering incentives, such as longer maternity leave, income support for every child, free kindergartens, and more after-school activities in elementary schools.[29] Efforts to increase fertility have also been made in Japan, Russia, Singapore, and Hong Kong, among other places. However, as yet, these efforts have not resulted in any noticeable change in birth rates, except in a few extreme cases, like Norway, where generous support to families with small children has increased the fertility rate to 1.8. But few other countries can afford to pay such large subsidies to those with small children.

Since we believe the world would be better with a smaller population, our not-so-surprising proposal is to encourage fewer children. We do not advocate removing the existing incentives that encourage people to choose to have more children (maternity and paternity leave, income support, and free kindergartens, for example), because they have many other advantages, but we do advocate the introduction of incentives to encourage people to have fewer children.

The simplest way to do this is to start celebrating families who already have fewer than two children. Instead of complaining that they are not doing their fair share to create the workforce of the future, we can pay a bonus to every woman who has had fewer than two children on her fiftieth birthday. In this way, the bonus will help strengthen the status of women and further increase their central importance in the crucial decision about family size. Why give this only to women? Women are obviously not the only segment of the population responsible for procreation, but they are the only ones who can actually carry and give birth to a child. This puts a pressure on women that men do not experience, and we see our proposal as a way to recognize that.

So we suggest a check for $80,000 per woman when they reach the age of fifty. This amounts to the GDP generated by an average rich-world citizen in two years. This idea can be defended in economic terms because these families have reduced their costs to the state—resulting in fewer kindergartens and schools, as well as a smaller burden on the health system—for all those years until their children would have started contributing to GDP. But the bonus is mainly in appreciation of those helping everyone to become more responsible planetary citizens.

We do not pretend that such a proposal will be easy to implement, or indeed easy to accept, especially as population growth is higher in the poor world than in the rich world. We accept, too, that there are all sorts of practical problems, such as how societies should reward singles, same-sex couples, the infertile, those who adopt children, and couples who have twins, triplets, or more when they planned for only one child.

What we are really trying to encourage here is a change in mindset—and for the rich world to lead by example. Societies everywhere need to recognize that there are too many people in the world and accept that it is a problem that needs to be fixed. Actually, societies need to accept that the problem will be fixed whether they like it or not. It can be fixed by nature or by choice.

We believe it is better for us to choose the way, and to make it as positive an experience as possible, rather than society having an abrupt correction forced upon it. Encouraging smaller families in the rich world through a financial incentive is one way to encourage this change in thinking.

13. INTRODUCE A GUARANTEED LIVABLE INCOME FOR THOSE WHO NEED IT MOST

As should be clear by now, the combined impact of our proposals for sharing work, boosting the pay of the unemployed, helping older people stay in work longer, paying those who work at home, using green stimulus packages, and offering bonuses for having fewer children would bring the rich world very close to paying every citizen a guaranteed fair income from cradle to grave. Our final suggestion is to make this explicit, though not for everyone. We propose a minimum livable income for all those in need—the elderly, disabled, sick, and unemployed.

We would have preferred to propose a minimum income for everyone. Unfortunately, back-of-the-envelope calculations (see below) show that this is simply not feasible at current income levels— even in the rich world.

Is it possible to pay a guaranteed income to all citizens in a modern society? And if so, how high could that income be?

A rich nation generates economic value per person of between $30,000 and $50,000 a year.[30] For simplicity, we will use an average of $40,000. If this were evenly distributed, each person (young, working age, old; man, woman, child) could receive $40,000 a year. A family of three would receive $120,000 a year.

That is a lot of money. And it shows that, theoretically, it is possible to pay each citizen $40,000 a year. Unfortunately, such a dramatic redistribution is not feasible. It would reduce the incentive to do any work and lead to a rebellion by the rich.

To pay $40,000 a year to everyone would require imposing high taxes (which would probably have to be progressive, rising with income) on those earning more than $40,000 a year, increasing the rate at which the rich would leave the country.[31] There would also have to be negative taxes (payment of the difference between actual income and $40,000 a year) for those earning less than $40,000 a year, as well as direct payments of $40,000 a year to those without an income (the young, old, sick or disabled, and unemployed).

Unfortunately, this is not possible in practice, because the current income distribution, though skewed, is not skewed enough. The Palma ratio (the share of income received by the richest 10% divided by the share of income received by the poorest 40%) ranges from 2.5 in poor countries to 1 in the OECD. This means that even halving the income of the top 10% would only increase the income of the poorest 40% by a quarter. The rich are not actually rich enough to make it possible to pay $40,000 to everyone every year, because there are so few of them. So redistribution can only be used to increase the incomes of a large minority but not to livable levels for all.

In that case, how much income transfer is actually possible? That depends on the answer to two questions:

1. How much do progressively higher income taxes reduce the willingness of rich people to work or even stay in the country?

2. What impact would a guaranteed minimum income have on the willingness of poor people to work for pay at all?

Such questions can only be answered by practical examples. The fate of the Soviet Union demonstrates that it is impossible (or at least extremely difficult) to run a system where everyone has the same income. But it is also an empirical fact that Nordic countries have been able to operate successfully for many decades with income taxes of up to 50% and state benefits to the elderly, sick, and unemployed of around $15,000 a year at a time when the GDP per person was around $40,000 a year.

The back-of-the-envelope calculation below shows what is possible.

In these Nordic countries, around 27% of the population (POP) are dependent (pensioners 15%, disabled 6%, sick 3%, unemployed 3%), and all receive around $15,000 a year.

So the total transfer is 27% x POP x $15,000 out of the total national income of 100% x POP x $40,000. In other words, around 10% of the total is taken from those who work and given to those who do not.

It appears, then, to be financially and practically possible to pay a guaranteed income equal to 40% of the GDP per person to 30% of the population. If $15,000 a year can be regarded as "livable" in societies where the average GDP is $40,000 a year, then it is possible to pay a livable minimum income to a third of the population—without going broke, inciting the rich to move abroad, or sparking a tax revolt. But that is probably the limit of what can be achieved, in our view.

The important conclusion to draw from the box above is that a transfer of 10% of GDP to those in need is feasible. It is possible to maintain a functioning modern economy when 10% of the total income is taken from those who work for a living and given to the elderly, disabled, sick, and unemployed.

Note that the beneficiaries of these welfare payments do not constitute a majority (they are only 27% of the population in the Nordic case), but they are still a big group. Note, too, that these Nordic countries levy additional taxes to pay for basic education and healthcare. If an individual wants more—be it pension, healthcare, or education—they are free to buy more using their after-tax income. Interestingly, this has not led to lower economic growth rates. The Nordic countries have achieved about the same rates of economic growth as less "socialistic" market economies—and they have remained competitive. The main reason appears to be the high levels of unionization and productive cooperation between business owners and workers, which has facilitated continuing restructuring of the economy.

There is, of course, a lot of administrative work involved in collecting taxes and providing the minimum income to the correct beneficiaries. So the question could be raised: Would it be more effective to simply pay a fixed minimum income to all citizens from cradle to grave, and then leave them to handle any periods of hardship they encounter? The administrative simplification would be enormous (our rough estimate is around 1% of GDP[32]).

We believe that the answer is no, it is not possible to transfer much more than around 10% of GDP from one group to another in this way. With a GDP per head of $40,000 a year, that would give everyone a meager $4,000 a year, which is not a livable income for anyone. It is not enough to maintain a decent level of well-being.

So our recommendation is to provide a guaranteed livable income to pensioners, the disabled, sick, and unemployed, with free healthcare and education paid directly by the state (using other budgets). The asylum problems in Europe in 2015 have also demonstrated that it is not politically sustainable to extend these rights to large numbers of immigrants.

So our thirteenth proposal is to provide a guaranteed minimum livable income for those who need it in the rich world at around a third of the average GDP per person. This is a realistic extension and completion of a system that is already emerging in many nations and moves somewhat closer to what John Maynard Keynes anticipated in his essay for his grandchildren. People may not be able to work only fifteen hours a week, as he hoped, but those who are able can probably eventually work something closer to an average of thirty hours a week and spend the rest of their time as they wish. And those who are unable to work would receive a third of the average national income.

We should point out at this stage that we are certainly not saying that the beneficiaries of a guaranteed minimum income should not also contribute actively to society. Those who are able should spend their work hours adding value in some way. We are not advocating a free ride.

Making a guaranteed livable income a legal right for those in need will make a huge difference in itself, however. For the employed, it will reduce the fear of losing one's job, especially in an era of rising robotization and mechanization. For the elderly, it will reduce the fear of ending life in economic misery. For the sick or disabled, it will reduce hardship.

A minimum livable income increases the dignity of a third of the population and helps reduce poverty and inequality instantly. Most importantly, it provides a big incentive for governments to redistribute the fruits of the coming technological revolution more fairly, to increase the pension age, and to implement many of our other proposals.

Like many other people, we believe that the provision of a guaranteed livable income will become inevitable. It is not a question of if but when. But we accept, too, that the change may have to be introduced gradually.

TOGETHER, OUR THIRTEEN proposals for a better world would reduce inequality, improve living standards for the majority of people in the rich world in the short term, and reduce greenhouse gas emissions. Most people would be much better off than if society continues down its current path.

Transferring income from the rich to the majority in conventional and unconventional ways is a major part of our proposal. But we are not suggesting that it is necessary to "eat the rich." Most people need an incentive—the possibility of becoming rich—to support positive economic and human development. Those who get rich, by addressing the problems and unsatisfied needs of society, should be allowed to keep enough of their wealth for a long enough time for them to enjoy it.

But that does not mean they should keep all their wealth, or that their children or family should inherit it when they die. And it certainly does not mean that they should be taxed less, just because they are rich, which is what happens in much of the world today. As we have shown, the idea that their wealth gradually trickles down to the poor in a free-market system is simply not true. Rather, it trickles upwards, increasing inequality, unless there is some sort of regulatory intervention. So we support wealth transfer, from rich to poor. No matter how leftist this might seem, it is a logical conclusion and a necessary response to the challenges the rich world is currently facing. In a stagnant economy it is not possible to increase demand without taking from the rich and giving to the majority. Similarly, it is not possible to reduce inequality without making the rich poorer and the poor a bit richer. And it is extremely difficult to reduce society's ecological footprint without sharing paid work and income more evenly.

There are, of course, many other possible suggestions we could have made to help humanity shift onto a more sustainable path, such as reform of the finance sector, halting agricultural subsidies, and curbing the lobbying power of businesses. We could have suggested reinventing the cooperative movement, scaling up grassroots initiatives, reforming company law to remove the right of many companies to have the legal status of people, changing the way economics is taught in schools and universities, and boosting basic research funding, especially in science and technology. All of these are more complex to implement (and some to understand), however, and would not offer change of the sort that benefits the majority of voters immediately. These ideas are, perhaps, for another time.

Although our proposals deliver a short-term advantage to the majority, they will not be easy to sell and get implemented, as we have already said. First, it will be necessary to explain to the majority that our proposals really are in their short-term interests. Second, it will be necessary to gather a majority in government to vote for change.

In this struggle it will be useful to have the assistance of additional indicators of human progress, to keep a closer eye on what is actually happening. As well as tracking GDP, society should measure average standards of health and education. It should monitor the Palma ratio, which measures the gap between rich and poor, and carefully watch the overall level of happiness, which some countries already do. When they make big economic decisions, governments should consider much more than they do today, such as poverty levels, the number of people in prison, and the rates of unemployment (and underemployment) in various societal groups. Society should track what is happening to average incomes and average costs, and monitor the levels of innovation and technological development, as well as their impact. Other indicators should include rates of social inclusion and participation, as well as levels of pollution and environmental degradation.

Much of this is already done, of course. But the results are not used enough in policy making, leaving society under the insidious influence of the mother of all modern-day indicators: the economic growth rate, or the rate of growth in GDP.

What human development indicators are currently measured, and what new ones should be added for a smooth transition to a better world?

The main indicators used to track human development today are the GDP growth rate (in % per year, in those sectors that are currently included in the GDP), the unemployment level (in % of those who have not yet given up looking for a job or been dropped from the statistics), consumer price inflation rates (in % per year), the central bank lending rate (in % per year), the trade surplus (in % of GDP), and the governmental surplus (in % of GDP).

Many of these are confusing to the layperson, especially as the last two are normally negative, indicating deficits year after year after year. (During the era of GDP growth this was actually not much of a problem, because the percentage remained reasonably stable.)

To better implement our thirteen proposals, it would help to track:

- The level of inequality (for example, measured as the ratio of the income going to the 10% richest citizens divided by the income going to the 40% poorest citizens in the nation—the Palma ratio).

- The greenhouse gas emissions per inhabitant (in tons of CO_2 equivalents per person per year)—ideally measured from the consumption point of view (the CO_2 embedded in what the average citizen consumes in a year) but at least from the production point of view (the CO_2 emitted from the activity inside the country's borders).

- The subjective well-being level (for example, measured as the fraction of the population who think things are getting better— who think there is progress). This can be measured by asking individual citizens if they believe that they are better off today than they were five years ago, and if they believe that they will be even better off five years in the future. If they answer "better, better," it can be said there is progress. If they answer "same, same," there is stagnation—though that may not indicate a problem if the level of well-being is already high. But if the current level of well-being is low, such stagnation signals lack of progress and the need for policy change.

If we were allowed to make only one adjustment to current indicators, it would be to supplement every mention of the growth rate in GDP with the growth rate in the percentage of the population who believes there is progress. In short, we would supplement "growth in GDP" with "growth in well-being," and remind people that if the first increases and the second declines, society is not on a good path.

CHAPTER 10

LET THE MAJORITY DECIDE

*In some allegedly democratic nations, the majority view
does not prevail. This will need to change if these societies are to
solve the problems of unemployment and inequality.*

T O HAVE A reasonable chance of being adopted, most of our proposed suggestions require a properly functioning democracy.
That might seem a simple enough requirement in most of the
developed world. Unfortunately, it is not.

The reason why adoption of our ideas requires a properly functioning democracy is that the world's business owners and the rich
will, understandably, challenge or resist many of our suggestions—
and aggressively. But a democratic majority can still win this battle,
much like it won the fight for improved healthcare, better schooling,
and more environmental protection in the last century, though it is
likely to involve a protracted struggle.

Success will depend on the democratic majority being able to
exercise their rights, to have their voices heard. This is a big assump-
tion, unfortunately, because, in much of the developed world, the
political and democratic systems are in crisis.

Although modern-day economists bind the ideas of the free market and democracy together tightly, as if they are part of the same
philosophy, this is not the case at all. In reality, the rule of the market
and democracy are mortal enemies, and to function efficiently, the
market has to emasculate the democratic process.

This is effectively what has happened in many parts of the world,
most notably in the United States, the U.K., Australia, and much of

the EU. Democracy has become little more than a word, a dogma, not a reality, and this makes it more difficult for our ideas to be introduced—though not yet impossible.

Although those in power always claim otherwise, they have long opposed democracy. In the eighteenth century, when modern democratic ideas first began to spread, the wealthy were greatly against giving the poor a say in how the world was run. It was felt that only the nobility were capable of running society; the rich fretted that if "the people" had a greater say, they would swiftly reform property laws and eradicate the rich's wealth.

Today, the rich have weakened the influence of government and greatly undermined the democratic process by manipulating the selection of political candidates and paying lobbyists to support their interests.

To divert attention, people have been told that it is economic growth and the market that drive social progress, because the market operates in their interests. Government is a barrier to progress, they are told. Only the market offers freedom, because only the market provides choice. In reality, of course, the market operates primarily in the interests of the companies that sell goods and services, and of their shareholders.

So it is the invisible hand and consumers' desire for lower prices that are blamed for children being forced to work for long hours in unsafe conditions in countries such as Bangladesh and Indonesia, but in reality, of course, it is companies that are driving this exploitation in order to meet shareholder demands for ever-rising corporate earnings. It is the unregulated nature of the market that has created the problem.

Similarly, because competition reduces corporate earnings, the choice of goods and services offered to consumers is much slimmer than it appears. Many business sectors are dominated by barely a handful of firms that sell goods and services under a variety of different brands to give an impression of consumer choice, and competition, which is no longer real.

Ideally, legislation would be used to curb the market power of these firms, and their shareholders, to ensure they operated in the interests of the majority, and certainly not against their interests. Governments would protect employees from exploitation wherever they were in the world, look after the environment, and foment genuine competition. Instead, people are told today that, to function properly, markets should never be controlled; they should be self-regulating. Government interference of any sort is portrayed as a bad thing. So attempts to regulate corporate activities are opposed not just by big business but also by those parts of the rich world's media that hold extreme free-market worldviews. Governments are frequently portrayed as incompetent, whereas the private sector is portrayed as efficient, even when big companies close and create unemployment, or destroy the environment, are corrupt, produce dangerous goods, or abuse monopoly power. To regulate business is portrayed as something wholly wrong. In contrast, the ideas of free markets and minimal regulation are presented as though they were fixed, as if they were laws of nature.

This process is strengthened by the manipulation of the democratic system so that it often seems to be little more than a source of entertainment. People are told about the benefits of free and fair elections, as if their vote will create a better future for the majority of the population. The reality is rather different, however, because in many rich-world countries, big business and rich individuals influence elections and laws to their advantage and suppress change. Nor does it even seem to matter anymore that promises made during elections are often impossible to deliver. Even in highly educated populations, millions of voters happily support proposals that are illogical or expressed in vague, abstract terms, such as the promise of "better government and lower taxes" or "change you can believe in." Millions more have become disenfranchised because they no longer believe the voting process will lead to a better world.

In well-running democratic systems, countries hold regular elections so that the people can elect representatives who will make decisions on their behalf. To prevent these representatives assuming too much power, there is a legal framework that establishes the principles any government must follow, and an independent judiciary.

There is a fair election process, open to everyone—or almost everyone (those who are too young, noncitizens, or suffer from certain types of mental illness are usually ineligible to stand, among others, as are those in prison or with criminal records, certainly in some countries). There are independent media, to ensure voters are properly informed, and freedom of association, meaning citizens have the right to form political groups and have their views heard, even if these views are seen as extreme by many people. Finally, citizens are educated and informed about their rights and civic responsibilities.

In many parts of the rich world, and indeed much of the poor world, those who are elected often pursue their own personal agendas, or look after the interests of lobby groups. Lobbyists, especially those representing big business, have become enormously powerful in Europe and the United States, influencing the selection of candidates, the outcome of elections, the role of the media, and legal processes in ways that the electorate cannot. Because big businesses tend to support right-leaning parties, the rich have been able to manipulate elections, without the voters understanding that the information being presented to them is frequently funded by someone with a specific, but usually undeclared, agenda.

As a consequence, the Western democratic system is sometimes little more than a sort of voting game, proclaimed as democratic without any proof that it is—because the proof is no longer available. As Francis Fukuyama argued in *The End of History and the Last Man*, the great passions that prompted armed struggles and tremendous acts of heroism in the twentieth century and before have been superseded by the market. Material improvement of the majority has given way to the hope of material gain by the individual. The democratic process has too often become a sideshow, while the market takes center stage.

The dogged pursuit of an extreme form of the free-market economic system and the necessary weakening of the democratic process for this to work have increased inequality in high-income societies and greatly silenced the voice of the people. It has also undermined the West's place in the world, because the rich world is perceived as pursuing an agenda that is entirely in its own interests and frequently against the interests of many millions of people in the poor world. The demand that poor countries should adopt the same extreme free-market system as the West has encouraged politicians of many poor nations to turn their countries into planet-ravaging, debt-driven, consumerist societies, too. The only holdouts are North Korea, Venezuela, Iran, Syria, and a few other countries, and they are publicly pilloried, subjected to economic sanctions, and demonized by the Western media as a consequence.

In the name of democracy, open trade, and the free market, the West has even encouraged civic resistance to lawfully elected governments in some countries[1] so that it can gain political influence as well as access to raw materials and markets. The same justifications are used to provide business opportunities for Western firms, which help convert these countries to free-market economies dominated by a financial elite. It is for these reasons, among others, that there is such anger in parts of the world, and such hatred toward the United States and the West in general. What has been imposed in the name of freedom and democracy has resulted in the disintegration of balanced societies, which has led to increased poverty (see Chapter 11), and the demand for ever greater output has led to widespread and unsustainable environmental destruction.

In many parts of the world, democracy has lost touch with its original meaning and purpose. Tied to the religion of economic growth, carried on the wings of the free market, democracy is sold as the answer to everyone's problems, when it has actually become a means for the rich to consolidate their income and power.

So if people want real change, they will first need a better system of democratic governance. Many hope that some sort of electoral reform, the banning of party financing, the public registration of lobbyists and ownership interests, and voter education will help. In our view, these changes are not nearly enough.

Since we believe that it is impossible to change the political system sufficiently in anything less than thirty years, we are constrained to working within the current imperfect system to encourage the introduction of legislation that will help boost the well-being of the majority. As we have said many times, this is why we have come up with proposals that we believe stand a good chance of surviving the current system, dominated as it is by short-termism and extensive political manipulation.

Our thirteen proposals are the most that can be done. Even then, success is not guaranteed, and the path to a better future will not be easy—as we freely acknowledge.

CHAPTER II

LET THE POOR WORLD GROW

*Our proposed approach to economic thinking will not be
needed in most of the developing world, where conventional
economic growth is still desirable. Rather, poor countries
should be helped to leapfrog the developed world.*

TRADITIONALLY, THE ECONOMIC systems adopted around the world have varied by political philosophy—communism vs. capitalism, for example—rather than by level of human development. The poor world has mostly followed the economic model of the richer world.

In what we are proposing, this will have to change, which makes sense because the development requirements of the poor world are completely different.

Populations in developing countries are rising, and will continue to rise for many years to come, meaning that consumption will have to increase and jobs will need to be created through economic growth. The vast majority of people in the poor world live on very low incomes, with hundreds of millions struggling to feed and clothe themselves. Industries are less developed, with many economies still based on resource extraction and agriculture. The impact of climate change will also become more obvious in much of the poor world sooner than in the rich world.

Although the rich world fulfills Keynes's idea of sufficient income for everyone to be able to work less and live well, this is not the case in the poor world. In the OECD, the challenge is one of redistribution, to share the available work and income more evenly so that everyone has enough. The high level of average income makes it politically feasible to start thinking about slowing the growth in output and consumption, to gradually reduce the ecological footprint, not only of the nation as a whole but of the average inhabitant. Rich-world societies can even increase well-being in the process: increased leisure time in return for lower consumption of resources.

In the poor world, it is basic economic development that is needed, and some of it is very basic indeed. To raise living standards in the poor world means increasing the output per person and distributing the benefits among the population. It means gradually increasing agricultural productivity so that more people can work in manufacturing, and then later in services. In short, it means good old-fashioned economic growth, ideally using the resource-efficient, clean technologies that have been developed in the rich world in recent decades.

Of course, a great deal can be achieved by redistribution in the poor world, too, because the gap between rich and poor is often even wider there than in the OECD. But the absolute numbers of poor people, as well as the practical barriers to achieving this sort of transfer, mean that any useful redistribution is likely to be postponed. Corruption is usually a bigger problem in the low-income world,[1] so the establishment of a properly functioning legal system would be much more beneficial to the well-being of the average citizen in the short term.

In the last thirty years, one developing country has stood out for what it has achieved economically. China's government has successfully shifted more people out of poverty in a shorter time than any other government in human history. It has done this in ways that are unorthodox and often difficult for other countries to replicate. In broad terms, China has followed in the footsteps of Japan and South Korea, both of which successfully moved from poor agriculture-based societies to postindustrial economies in less than fifty years. To achieve this, both required a solid dose of central planning. Both were also developed by a small elite, who followed a clear plan. They did not develop by focusing on what was most profitable in the short term, or on what the majority preferred.

China's development has required a single-mindedness from the government and the people, as well as the will to exploit the opportunity that emerged when the rich world pursued its market ideology to the point that most of the simple manufacturing was moved from the West to China. The Chinese were smart enough, and sufficiently well organized, to keep a large share of the profits from this transfer, thereby building huge international reserves. While the rich world went on a borrow-and-spend spree, China supplied the goods, though the environmental cost has been horrendous.

However, this book is not about the policy changes needed to help the poor world make the transition to a healthier economic system. This book is about the rich world. What we can say, though, is that the developing world will need forward-looking policies, too, to allow economies to grow, raise standards of living, and protect infant industries. To meet the world's environmental goals, notably on climate change, poor countries will also need a rapid transition to an energy system not based on fossil fuels.

Here, the rich world can help—by offering leapfrogging technologies that would allow poor countries to build a renewable low-emission energy network using the latest engineering. In the long run, this is in everyone's interests. To make it happen quickly, the rich world would need to pay the extra costs involved to provide the low-carbon energy systems (solar panels, windmills, hydroelectric dams, and biomass-based energy plants). This would give rich-world firms a market for their high-tech energy products and the poor world an energy system that does not worsen the climate. In our view, this should be funded by the rich world, because it is in humanity's interests, and because most of the greenhouse gases that exist in the atmosphere today are the result of the rich world's past economic development and current consumption. Such magnanimity is unlikely, however, as the rich world's taxpayers are not likely to be supportive. This is true, unfortunately, even if development assistance is used to pay for manufacturing these low-carbon energy systems in the rich world, with the work done by the rich world's workers and by businesses controlled by the rich world's shareholders.

The most fundamental problem facing the poor world is the fact that the planet is too small, or more accurately, that humanity has allowed itself to become too big for the planetary resource base. At current resource intensity (tons used per product) and current emissions intensity (tons emitted per product), it will be extremely difficult for more than a third of the world's population to achieve the same living standards as exist in the United States or Europe today, and it would require decades of technological advances for the entire human population to reach the same level. Even for China—with 1.3 billion people—to attain the same standard of living as the OECD today—with a total of 1 billion people—would require a second planet's worth of natural resources and pollution absorption capacity, with current levels of technology.[2]

The good news is that it is actually possible to advance technology sufficiently to allow everyone to live well within the boundaries of the planet. The challenge is to do it fast enough so that it more than counterbalances the combined growth in population and the increase in footprint per person.

When it comes to energy, for example, there is already enough installed capacity around the world to ensure that 7 billion people can live pleasant enough lives.[3] Existing energy capacity mainly burns fossil fuel, so the question is how fast can it transition to renewable resources without society having to scrap the installed capacity before the end of its lifetime? Rough estimates show that this could be done over fifty years and at comparatively little cost—just 1% of GDP a year. The real problem is that low-carbon electricity generation is generally more expensive than today's fossil-based electricity, so the transition is almost impossible in unregulated free-market economies.

But it *is* possible. Earth receives ten thousand times as much energy from the sun every day as would be required by 7 billion people using as much power as present-day Europeans. So it is possible to have a world without greenhouse gas emissions, a world that runs on electricity for transport, air conditioning/heating, manufacturing, and everything else. Even when it is dark, there can be sufficient energy, because surplus electricity accumulated during the day can be converted into hydrogen and burned as clean fuel during the night. The solution is there. The trouble is that society is not currently willing to pay the small additional cost.

In our view, the poor world should seek to improve the lot of its population by using whatever means necessary. It should pursue conventional economic growth, learning from those nations that are already ahead in the game of increasing the GDP per person. Developing countries should also strive to use the most energy- and climate-efficient technologies possible, and have these subsidized by the rich world if they can. We also think they should follow the example of China and seek to limit their populations, not with a one-child policy necessarily but through improved education and health, more easily available contraception—and ideally, by paying a bonus to those families who have had fewer than two children.

To us, the rich world has a moral obligation to help and to pay for as much of this development as possible—particularly when it comes to the provision of low-carbon electricity—because the really huge step up for people in the developing world comes with access to power. Access to electric power increases levels of well-being immediately and is something the rich world could provide.

The poor world will need to manage some extremely complicated people and money flows in the process of its development, of course. It will need to facilitate a huge exodus of people and investment from agriculture to manufacturing and then services, as well as an enormous flow from villages to megacities. It will also need to organize its workforce to supply the services (education, health, and elderly care) that constitute the core of modern well-being. It should seek to do what Japan, South Korea, Singapore, and China have already achieved: to quadruple the GDP per person over thirty years. If the poor nations could do this, they would become able to provide each citizen with a reasonable standard of living.

This is a huge challenge, but it is doable—as illustrated by those nations that already have moved briskly from agricultural to industrial economies. However, it will be extremely difficult for other developing nations to make the transition with open trade and an unregulated market-based economic system.

In our view, the poor world would make its development much easier if it chose to distance itself from extreme free-market thinking. Developing countries should try to be smarter because, just as the extreme free-market model has not created enough work in the rich world and has widened inequality, it has not done what it promised in the poor world in the last thirty years either. Here, too, it has increased inequality.

Developing country governments need to understand that another of the central pillars of the gospel of extreme free-market thinking is flawed. This is the belief that conventional free-market economics has lifted a billion people out of poverty over the last thirty years.

It is simply not true.[4] The heavy lifting was actually done by China.

The bare facts are not questioned. According to the U.N., the number of people living on an income of $1.25 a day fell by just over 1 billion between 1990 and 2015, from 1.9 billion people to 836 million.[5] Both the World Bank and IMF, strong supporters of the free-market model, have published similar statistics.

These claims have several problems, however. First, they give the misleading impression, backed up by triumphant reports and newspaper headlines, that free-market economics is the route out of poverty and misery. They also suggest that most of these 1 billion people have been moved out of poverty completely, that there is no longer any need to worry about them, because the system has already set them on a new and better path.

In truth, nearly 90% of the developing world's population still live on less than $10 a day. More than half live on less than $2.50 a day. The gap between rich and poor has also grown, and the gap between the rich world and the poor world is much bigger than it was three decades ago. In fact, it is wider today than it was in 1820.[6] The consolidated figures published by the U.N. also mask what is happening nationally and regionally. In some parts of the world, notably most of sub-Saharan Africa, the share of the population living on $1.25 a day has barely changed at all, despite thirty years of global economic growth. Just under 60% of the world's extremely poor live in a handful of very populous countries—India, Bangladesh, Nigeria, Congo—where little has changed in thirty years.

Most critically, most of the progress in the last thirty years was in just one country: China. By taking China out of the statistics and raising the poverty threshold to $2.50 a day, the percentage of people in the world who can be classified as living in poverty did not change at all between 1980 and 2005.[7] Half of the world lived in poverty in 1980 and half of the world lives in poverty today. There has been no reduction at all. Raising the barrier to $2.50 a day also makes sense. The level that defines poverty was set at $1 a day in 1980 by the World Bank. It was raised to $1.25 in 2008 to "take account of inflation." Yet the change did not properly take account of inflation, as $1 in 1980 was actually equal to $2.61 in 2008. Setting the barrier at $1.25 today means it is much lower than it was in 1980, which means many fewer people are included. This greatly explains why the number of people living in poverty appears to have declined. Using the 2015 equivalent of a 1980 dollar—$2.90—as the poverty threshold reveals that the percentage of people living in poverty in the world has actually *increased* slightly in the last thirty-five years.

There is also concern about how poverty statistics are collected, because the poorest people in any society are most often those who are homeless and unregistered. They are the people whom the U.N.'s researchers will have the greatest difficulty reaching. This suggests that even the official figures are likely to be understated.

Indeed, there is huge uncertainty in these data, as in all social statistics, despite the fact that they are often provided to four or more significant digits. It is actually impossible to know the population of many places, let alone their incomes, to more than two significant digits, because more than one hundred developing countries do not have a functioning system to measure birth and death rates, and twenty-six have not collected data on infant mortality since 2009.[8] In reality, only 20% of births in the world occur in countries with proper civil registration systems. Even in the United States, the population is counted only once every ten years, and even there to an error level of around 0.1%, which is equal to plus or minus 300,000 people. Finally, the GDP numbers issued by the U.N., World Bank, and others are often adjusted for PPP. This is to make allowances for relative currency rates and different costs of living, to try to make the numbers easier to compare, because what you can buy with a dollar in New York is different from what you can buy with a dollar in Mogadishu. But using PPP also distorts the numbers, making incomes in the poor world appear better and those in the rich world worse. India's nominal average income doubles when it is translated into PPP terms, for example, whereas that of Denmark is almost halved.

Of course, using PPP is certainly better than using local currency units, or local currency translated into dollars at current exchange rates, because the costs of living *do* vary enormously. It is important to remember the limitations of this approach, however.

Despite all these problems with the official statistics and with how poverty is measured, society's lack of specific knowledge does not diminish the central goal: to improve the average well-being of all inhabitants on the planet. The lack of precise data only makes the task more complex.

Another way to help the poor world move in a better direction faster would be to transfer some of the wealth of the rich world. As with our other suggestions, this can be achieved in ways that need not be very disruptive if it is done gradually.

As we have already suggested, one of the simplest ways to achieve this would be for the rich world to build low-carbon energy systems in the poor world, and then to give away the electricity. Slightly less Utopian would be for the rich world to build the utilities and sell the electricity, but on deferred payment conditions. The rich world could ask to be paid back once the recipient countries had reached a certain level of economic development, in terms of GDP per person, for example. If a recipient country managed its development well, it could probably start paying its energy bills in forty years—which would conveniently help to pay for rising pension costs in much of the rich world. But since this idea involves a lower return on investment than could be achieved by spending the money elsewhere, the chances are low that rich-world populations would be so magnanimous. So we are stuck with the current situation where the only thing the rich world is willing to do is *lend* money to poor countries—at near-commercial rates—to build the utilities needed to lift them out of poverty and thereby also shackle them with debt. As with so much else we have discussed, the long-term consequence of this approach is that income and wealth again flow from the poor to the rich.

Income redistribution from the rich world to the poor world could be achieved in other ways, of course, if the rich world were willing to go along with it. It is perfectly possible for the rich world to continue to live well, and more efficiently than now, and offer the poor world a more acceptable average standard of living. Such a transfer would re-balance wealth, reduce emissions, cut resource use, and, because even slightly richer people tend to have fewer children, slow the rate of population growth. We acknowledge, however, that this is unlikely to happen to any significant degree at all. Most people in the rich world are already too tied up with their own problems to think much about those who are even worse off in distant lands.

CHAPTER 12

SAVING THE WORLD

*Our approach will increase average well-being,
slow resource destruction, cut greenhouse gas emissions,
and reduce environmental damage.*

I N 1972, WHEN *The Limits to Growth* was first published, its authors—including one of us—believed it would be relatively simple to avoid the looming social and ecological threats. All that was required was a self-imposed limitation on the material consumption of the world's citizens once an acceptable standard of living had been achieved. The lower the global population, the higher this standard of living could be.

That advice was largely ignored, however, so humanity is now in ecological overshoot.

Overshoot is a situation whereby people use more resources than are being regenerated by nature, or emit more pollution than nature can absorb. There is overshoot when:[1]

1. there is a rising accumulation of waste and pollutants;
2. there are falling stocks of groundwater, forests, fish, and soils;
3. capital, labor, and energy are increasingly being used to compensate for what were once free natural services (neutralization of sewerage, flood control, air purification);
4. there is a need for more frequent repair of the physical infrastructure; and
5. there is increasing conflict over resources.

Overshoot has occurred because global society has been pushing too hard on the economic gas pedal for nature to cope, and because there are too many people in the world for current human technology to allow us to live cleanly. The consequence is that humanity's negative impact on the planet is becoming too great, so the physical conditions—the framework around society—are deteriorating.

The simplest thing to do, of course, would be to stop the destructive activity—to cut resource use and damaging emissions—until these fall below the sustainable carrying capacity of the planet again. But history shows that this is not as easy as it might sound.

During the last fifty years or so, technological developments mean that it has been possible to keep the average ecological footprint per person more or less constant. But the human population has risen, so the total ecological footprint has increased to 1.5 times the current carrying capacity of the planet.[2] That is, humanity is living as if there were 1.5 planets. This is not sustainable, certainly not in the long term.

One of the most obvious consequences of human overshoot is climate change. Because humanity emits twice as much CO_2 each year as is being absorbed by the oceans and terrestrial plants and soil, the difference is accumulating in the atmosphere and will remain there for hundreds of years. With this increasing concentration come unavoidably higher temperatures and ever-weirder weather.

This problem will continue to worsen until emissions are reduced to zero. Even then, global society will still be stuck with temperatures above normal—and the associated extreme weather and rises in sea level—for centuries. In other words: continued climate overshoot will reduce well-being to an ever-greater degree.

So there is a need for humanity to change. If it does not, then nature will force change upon society—and nature's way is likely to be less attractive than the human-made variety.

When faced with the evidence of these problems, many people remain sanguine. They believe that technology will provide the solution, that tomorrow's scientists will discover the necessary answers. This thought is comforting, but it is also unrealistic and unjustified, mainly because it is not different technology that is needed but the willingness to use what we already have. Humanity could begin to solve the climate problem today by shifting to sustainable ways of producing low-carbon energy and food. The technologies are already available. What is missing is the willingness to change, to accept solutions that are more expensive than now.

But what will happen if there is no deliberate change?

The simple answer is that there will be a collapse, though what we mean by this requires some explanation.

The collapse we anticipate, and want to help humanity avoid, will not manifest as a sudden crisis. It will not be triggered by some unexpected event that changes almost everything overnight, or even over a year, with living standards abruptly pushed back to those of the Dark Ages. Human history and major environmental or social change does not happen like that. Big changes take many years. It takes time for social and political pressures to build, for a transition to begin, and for the long-term effects to become clear. The French and Russian revolutions, the two world wars of the twentieth century, and even the 2008 financial crisis were not distinct historical events with clear beginnings and obvious endings. All were parts of a long tumbling series of changes and social conflicts, many of which had roots that stretched back decades. All had major social and economic implications that lasted for many years afterwards, too.

What we define as collapse is a situation where more than half of the rich people in the world lose most of something they value over a period of less than twenty years, against their wishes.[3] (We have chosen to not define collapse by its impact on the poor world because, to varying degrees, social and economic collapse is already a reality for the world's billions of poor, many of whom suffer disproportionately from the current economic system and the early consequences of climate change.)

Collapse is when there is a substantial (more than 50%) loss or decline in something those in the rich world hold dear—their assets, incomes, job prospects, health, security, or their freedom to travel, enjoy untouched nature, or express themselves, for example. In emotional terms, it is when the rich world's population can look back, quantitatively and qualitatively, and see that the past was better than the present. We do not regard it as collapse if this decline or loss was planned, if societies chose to cut back deliberately for their own good.

Collapse of this sort is very difficult to perceive, even when it is happening. Like the decay of a personal relationship, the sort of collapse we are talking about only becomes obvious to most people long after it has started.

In our view, there is considerable evidence to suggest that the type of collapse we fear, the sort that was anticipated in *The Limits to Growth* nearly forty-five years ago, is already under way. Climate change is perhaps the most obvious sign, and is a direct consequence of too many human emissions. But the migration problems in many parts of the world—the rising number of conflicts, increasing species loss, oceanic acidification, overpopulation, and growing restrictions on personal freedom—are all signals, too. They are the result of excessive material consumption in the rich world, of humanity pushing beyond the boundaries of sustainability.

These disruptions are not just warning signals, however, they are the start of the fraying of the current world order, of human society coming apart at the seams. The greatest need today is to stop the process from becoming self-reinforcing, leading to the almost complete dismantling of the great edifice that human society has so ardently built for so long.

What we are saying in this book is that it is not too late to avoid the worst, even now. The environmental situation will certainly worsen in the next few decades because there are so many lags in the system. But it is still possible to shift society onto a better economic path and avoid something much more serious. It is still possible to shift humanity away from a resource-intensive economic growth model to one that is in balance with nature, where there is a fairer distribution of incomes and work and a higher average level of well-being—everywhere. Humanity can do a great deal in the next couple of decades to make the necessary transition to a better system, though there is no doubt that they will be stormy.

The thirteen proposals we have made offer a conduit—a set of actions that can take the rich world in a better direction, with minimal disruption to the majority of citizens. Shifting to a life with less work, with more of a social safety net, and with higher taxes on resources and business would also reduce raw materials use. This would lead to lower greenhouse gas emissions and gradually stop further environmental damage.

We acknowledge, of course, that the implications of the changes we are proposing will be wide ranging. As well as sharing work and income more, societies will need to:

- cut back damaging industries and develop clean ones;
- reduce resource use and pollution, especially in the rich world; and
- move toward circular economies, with greater recycling and sharing.

The sector of the economy that has to shrink most is the fossil energy business. It will actually have to be removed from the surface of the planet. This will not happen fast (but, we believe, by the year 2100 the fossil business will be history), because the transition will be resisted fiercely by those who work in the oil, coal, and gas business, as well as those who own it.

Perhaps society needs something like an Energy Truth and Reconciliation Commission, where those who carry so much responsibility for the climate problems are given the chance to talk about what they have done before they move on to new careers with their dignity intact. Even without this, though, society will need to bring together the owners and workers of all the big oil, coal, and gas firms, get them to accept that they are the cause of a very big problem, thank them for generating the energy that the world needed and consumed for decades, and then help them find new jobs.

At the same time, society will need to help renewable energy businesses grow. As much of the traditional energy business is still heavily subsidized, this sets a helpful precedent. It makes it easier to argue that the state should subsidize future forms of energy, too, to ease the transformation and ensure renewables are able to compete with destroyables.

This shift from dirty to clean energy will not mean fewer jobs, as we have tried to explain. It will certainly lead to lower consumption, but the total number of jobs will stay constant. The jobs will simply move from dirty industries to clean ones. Instead of working on oil rigs and down coal mines, people will make solar panels, produce fuel cells, and maintain windmills and hydropower systems.

This shift would obviously be unwelcome to those who work in the traditional energy sector, as they would need to retrain. But structural changes like this have happened many times before, and they have not been too onerous. Once there were horses for transport and people who tended gas lamps in the streets. Now there are cars and electric lighting. Once there will have been oil and coal, and then there will be solar, hydrogen, and wind power. As long as the transition is not too fast, and people have time to adapt, it should not be too difficult, especially in rich countries, which can pay the unemployed adequately and retrain those who need it.

The financial cost of phasing out the fossil business would be very high, of course, as most of the coal, oil, and gas currently in the ground would have to stay there. As well as dismantling the physical infrastructure, many companies would also have to write off trillions of dollars of booked assets, to the chagrin of their shareholders. Society would need to replace hundreds of millions of fossil-fuel vehicles with low-carbon vehicles, too. As long as this was all done in a planned and gradual way, however, the costs, though high, would be a tiny fraction of the total economic muscle of modern society. Just a 1% shift in economic activity each year for a generation would be enough.

The transition would also be extremely troublesome for any fossil-based business that resisted change, that clung on for too long, especially because the financial payback times in the oil and gas business are often very long. Companies that try not to change risk having to abandon their investments long before they reach the end of their productive lives. Many other types of business, as well as many national governments, risk running into the same difficulty.

It is important to distinguish here between physical costs and those that are merely financial. The first group carries human and environmental implications. The latter is simply a loss of paper value and leads primarily to a reduction in the wealth of shareholders. Although this is bad for the rich, it increases equality—without any loss of productive capacity.

A successful transition would also involve cutting back all those other industries that depend on carbon-based energy, or shifting them toward other sources of power. Making cars, airplanes, trains, ships, and trucks run with 100% renewable energy would take some time, of course, but we believe it will happen this century, by shifting to electricity, hydrogen (which is nothing but stored electricity), and some biofuels. It could actually happen quite quickly, if society so wished.

It is already possible for car makers to produce vehicles that run on low-carbon fuels, and as long as the fuels are generated cleanly, the emissions are zero. Even if the power is not generated cleanly—and during the transition period—any emissions from these vehicles will be concentrated in a small number of locations, namely the power plants, and so can be cleaned up much more easily than the exhausts of hundreds of millions of traditional cars.

A forward-looking society could do much more to accelerate the necessary mobility transition, though. A glance at the streets of most cities makes it clear that cars are not used as much as they could be. Many sit parked by the road or in garages most of the time. A great deal could be achieved, therefore, by making them easier to share (as many cities have already demonstrated). If car makers were also persuaded (with the help of some legislation) to design cars to last longer, which is not technically difficult, it would be possible to reduce the number of vehicles on the roads and the number produced each year by more than half. That may not be good for the car business, or the steel, glass, and plastics industries. But it would be very good for the human ecological footprint and greatly help the transition to a more sustainable world.

The same thinking, the same opportunities, and the same constraints apply to many other industries. Manufacturers could easily produce washing machines, lightbulbs, and refrigerators that last for decades rather than continuing to take the current approach, which is known as "planned obsolescence," where the lives of products are deliberately shortened to encourage replacement sales. It is easily possible to reduce the amount of packaging consumed, too, to design mobile phones modularly so that elements can be upgraded, and to build houses and offices that generate power instead of using it. There are hundreds of ways to make the world better by reducing demand for the items people do not really need and by providing encouragement, through the tax system, to businesses that are not ecologically destructive.

A great deal can also be achieved through recycling and increasing efficiency. This will be essential, in fact, because many of the easiest-to-access and highest grades of many metals and ores have already been mined, with the consequence that what remains will become more difficult and more expensive to extract, and their quality will decline. Recycling is not always possible, of course—it is only practical and economical for a limited number of raw materials because many are permanently altered when they are used, changed into gases, or combined with other chemicals in ways that make it impossible for them to be recovered. In the short term, societies can achieve much by recycling used products more, however. In the long term, manufacturers will need to design products and manufacturing methods that simplify the recycling process to make it more attractive and more practical.

As well as recycling more and increasing efficiency, societies can break the current destructive cycle by adopting the principles of the circular economy.

In the circular economy, most commonly used items are reused, repaired, or refurbished, and designed with this in mind. Many are also shared. Again, for most of us, this would have very little obvious negative impact. So long as the transition is managed and gradual, it would lead to only slightly slower growth in consumption, and a slightly faster pace of economic restructuring. The latter is, of course, bad for those who would lose their jobs, notably in the fast-moving consumer goods industries. But the first—slower growth in consumption—hardly matters in rich-world societies, especially if everyone is in the same boat.

Thankfully, a circular economy does not mean fewer jobs. Rather, the opposite. An analysis done for the Club of Rome[4] underlines the benefits of shifting into a circular economy, demonstrating that it is possible to reduce damaging emissions and create jobs at the same time. In essence, jobs are shifted from the production of consumer goods and services to the production of a cleaner environment. Already, hundreds of companies have adopted the principles, because they actually make good business sense.

Simply making products last longer and reducing people's hunger to replace what they own so frequently would have a huge impact on society and the human ecological footprint. Not only is it then possible to reduce the quantity of goods consumed, but an entirely new business sector would emerge to repair, upgrade, and remodel items, creating millions of new jobs. Better still, these would be local and often highly skilled jobs, not repetitive and poorly paid factory jobs, which can easily be robotized. With less need to ship goods around the world, the circular economy also cuts energy use and emissions. But as we have stated many times over, the cost of this saner world is slower consumption—and hence resisted by many.

As will be obvious at this stage, most of what we are proposing requires more government intervention, something that many people might consider undesirable and unlikely when there is so much political and economic pressure to move in the opposite direction today, to make government smaller. This negative view of governance and regulation will eventually have to change, however, though it is likely to take Tolstoy's two great warriors—patience and time.

A change in mindset about the role of the state will be necessary for many reasons. Aging populations will bring governments many new challenges, stretching medical and care budgets. Rising immigration—because of economic opportunity, conflict, and climate change—will increase the political heat, too, while new technologies will boost the numbers of the jobless, unless regulators step in to manage the transition. The invisible hand will become rather lame over the next two decades, in other words, forcing those with a political mandate to intervene more.

The biggest reason for greater government intervention in the future, however, will be climate change. Only the state will be able to direct the repair and adaptation work that will be needed to counteract climate damage. Walls will have to be built to protect towns from rising sea levels and more frequent storms, and new houses will be needed for the permanently displaced. Roads and other essential infrastructure will also have to be strengthened to withstand different rainfall patterns and temperatures. Those who do the construction work will need to be paid for this, and the only source of such funds will be the state.

We will discuss the role of government and the implications of this change in the next, and final, chapter.

CHAPTER 13

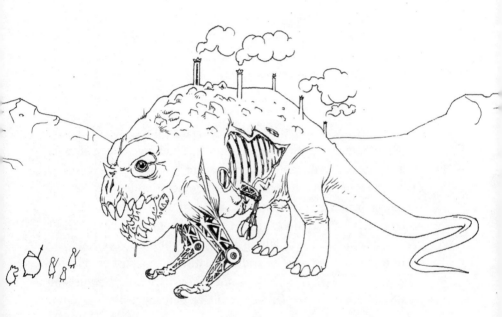

THE EPIC BATTLE TO COME

The transition from a moribund economic system to a sustainable one will be the epic social, political, and environmental battle of the twenty-first century, and the stakes are high.

THE FUNDAMENTAL DILEMMA facing humanity is not difficult to grasp. Society can either let the current economic system impose its relatively predictable and unpleasant long-term consequences, or it can choose an alternative path. The decision will be the epic social, environmental, and political battle of the twenty-first century, and the stakes are as high as they can ever be: modern civilization's continued existence in anything like its current form.

In this book, we have provided a pathway to a sustainable economic system, a transition that is not overly disruptive, because our proposals can be implemented gradually. Our suggestions also provide immediate benefits to the overwhelming majority of people in the rich world today. At the very least, we hope our ideas might stimulate some sensible discussion and debate about the best way forward, though after a great deal of hard and heavy thinking, we can see no other obvious, less disruptive, alternative route.

It would certainly be foolish to continue on the current path, because unemployment will remain high or become higher, inequality will rise further, conventional economic growth will gradually stall, and climate change will steadily worsen. We can say all this with certainty. The only way to avoid this future is to gradually shift to another economic system, one that is fairer and more sustainable.

By this stage, it will have become obvious, too, we hope, that the necessary transition will not happen by itself. It will require greater government intervention in markets and society. The free market cannot solve today's social problems, nor can big business, the Church, or the many thousands of grassroots initiatives. Government will have to play a substantially bigger role if humanity is to avoid collapse.

Calls for a stronger state are typically met with the response that such ideas hark back to a failed Soviet era. Free-market economists dismiss demands for greater state intervention by pointing out that this has been tried before and that it simply does not work.

That is not what we are talking about at all, though. We are not advocating a return to something that has failed. We are offering a range of proposals that we know will work, because they have already worked in other places. But they also require more active state intervention.

Most people would surely agree that Soviet communism did not work in the Eastern Bloc during the twentieth century. It is also true, though, that although U.S.-style capitalism increased average living standards in the rich world for a while, it is not boosting them anymore. It has also led to an ever-increasing concentration of wealth and unsustainable environmental damage. In other words, Soviet government did not work, but small government does not lead to a Utopia either—except for a privileged few. It is also a fact that Japan and South Korea succeeded in raising the well-being of their populations to an impressive degree during the second half of the twentieth century through active state planning. Similarly, the Communist Party of China is well on its way to replicating this success through centralized direction and control.

There is a strong voice from proponents of the free-market system that argues that almost any sort of state intervention in the market is bad and that government, in almost any form, is a menace. Ronald Reagan was famous for his strong dislike of big government, and his views have remained fashionable.

Yet government is not bad. It is poorly run government that is bad.

Over the last thirty years, the rich world—and much of the poor world—has been drip-fed a message that says that governments are almost always incompetent and are filled with paper-pushers who slow progress and tie up businesses with red tape. People are told that it is free enterprise that works, that lean, competitive businesses make the best decisions. Competition and the profit motive are what work.

In truth, of course, governments around the world make good decisions all the time. They are responsible for most of the infrastructure that exists, for the roads, bridges, and airports that allow economies to function. They are responsible for much of the legal system, for defense, and for many essential international agreements. When it comes to technology, it was government funding that paid for the development of the jet engine, the international space station, and the Internet. Governments run most of the schools, universities, and hospitals in the world, too.

Governments do lots of good things.

Businesses also do lots of bad things. Companies are not always efficient and good. They often make bad investment decisions, and they frequently go bust, sometimes with very damaging social and financial consequences. It is businesses that sell food that makes people obese, promote ideas that make young women sick, restrict the sale of medicines that could save lives, overfish seas, and pollute the atmosphere—and they would do all of these to an even greater degree were they not restricted in their activities by government regulation.

It is not government that is the problem per se. It is weak government that is the problem, and a political system that hinders reform.

Neither Adam Smith nor the nineteenth-century classical political economists were the dogmatic champions of laissez-faire economics they are often portrayed as in historical and contemporary literature. Within the system of what Smith called "natural liberty," he said there needed to be a balancing mechanism for keeping individual self-interest from becoming destructive. Although Smith was more suspicious of a government's capacity for adequately managing economic affairs than we are, he also recognized that markets should not operate in the absence of government. He saw the market as a tool for allocation, which could function efficiently only within a framework of legal, political, and moral constraints.[1]

We acknowledge that government departments can be slow moving and the people who work within them are often badly paid. This needs to change. Public sector pay should reflect the importance of government to society, and if there cannot be high pay, there should be other benefits for working in public bureaucracies—in addition to the pleasure of knowing that those who are employed there are creating a better world.

Promoting the best people to work in government is perfectly possible. For most of the last two thousand years, China has sought out the best talent for its Mandarins and has always carefully trained those it selects to run government departments and institutions properly. It pays bureaucrats well, too, because the job they do is openly acknowledged to be valuable and important. Other Asian countries, notably Singapore, take a similar tack, recruiting and training the best people to work for the state.

To us, it seems obvious that if there are smart, competent, well-remunerated, socially ambitious people in the public sector, they are much more likely to make good, socially beneficial decisions.

As well as increasing the role of governments, it would be better, in our view, if the world's nations could agree on some sort of global governance system to handle the biggest challenges more effectively—to address climate change, solve migration problems, and diffuse conflict. That may be a hope too far, but effective global governance is something that will be needed more, not less, in the decades ahead.

As well as strengthening the role of government, there needs to be a change in the dominant social philosophy, in the way people view the world.

For the last forty-odd years, four basic tenets have dominated Western social thinking: freedom of the individual, free markets and open trade, minimal government influence, and sufficient military strength to defend the nation's security.

These served the majority of people well for a while, when increasing output brought indisputable advantage. But those days are gone. Today, the main challenges are unemployment, unfair income distribution, and environmental decline.

As a consequence, we believe that society should now promote four different ideas. Rather than regarding the individual as sacrosanct, societies and economic systems should boost average well-being. Rather than leaving markets to run themselves, they should be managed and operated in the interest of society, even if this means restricting trade. And, as we have said, rather than promoting small government, the state should be right-sized and properly supported to tackle the challenges that lie ahead. Finally, rather than building greater military defenses, the goal should be to protect collective well-being, to promote the highest quality of life for as many people as possible, within the bounds of what the planet can support.

In short, societies in both the rich world and poor should rediscover one of the central tenets of traditional economics, as it was once taught: the efficient management of scarce resources to achieve the best possible outcome for the largest number of people—with due respect for nature.

What does it mean to shift from extreme free-market thinking to modified market thinking?

OLD THINKING	NEW THINKING
Freedom of the individual	Fulfilled individuals
Free markets and free trade	Managed markets and sufficient trade
Small government	Right-sized state
Strong defense	Defense of collective well-being

Different economic thinking will be needed to restructure rich-world societies so that they operate for the benefit of the majority, not just the richest 1%. To do this means that free-market ideas of minimal regulation, open trade, and competition that leads to the survival of the fittest are no longer useful. To encourage "survival of the fittest" is, in any case, and like so many free-market economic ideas, a reinterpretation of what was originally intended. When nineteenth-century biologists such as Darwin (who did not actually coin the phrase—it was Herbert Spencer) talked about the "fittest," they did not mean "competitive, lean, sporty, and strong," which is how the idea is portrayed by many economists today. They actually meant "that which fits best." It is the life-forms that "fit" their environment best that survive.

And this is exactly what we hope will happen to the human race during the twenty-first century: it will learn to "fit" the world better by successfully developing an economic system that can address the challenges of unemployment, inequality, and above all, the threat of accelerating climate change.

It is much the same with many of the ideas of Adam Smith, incidentally, many of which have also been warped by modern-day interpretations. Smith thought that economies should be developed not to make people rich but to raise average living standards and improve the lot of the poor. When he talked about the "invisible hand" and people acting in their own "self-interest," he believed that this would benefit society as a whole and raise living standards for everyone. He was not advocating selfishness or minimal regulation.

With today's extreme free-market ideology, individual self-interest and the market have been left to make the big decisions. But as we have explained, although decisions made this way were good for a while, they are not good for the majority any longer, and they have substantial downsides for future generations and nature. This approach increases unemployment, inequality, and poverty, while creating environmental havoc.

Defining what societies should do instead is not very difficult. As well as having enough food and some sort of meaningful employment, people need decent housing, equal access to good-quality education, enough leisure time to enjoy their lives, enlightening and inspiring sources of entertainment, and adequate healthcare. Societies need to be fair, and people should be treated equally as well as with respect. Human progress should not involve wrecking the environment either, because other species have a right to prosper, too.

The biggest barrier to society achieving this transformation is *not* economic. It is political. Creating a better world is a political decision, not an economic one. It is a question of organization. There are enough resources and productive capacity, the right technology, and sufficient accumulated wealth on the planet for people to make the necessary transition—even with a population of more than 7 billion—and for everyone to live adequately. The rich would need to live less flamboyantly than now, of course, but we are doubtful that the transition would reduce their overall well-being very much.

The thirteen proposals explained in this book would shift today's moribund rich-world economic system to one that is more sustainable, with increased well-being as the reward for the majority.

To us, and we hope also to you by now, it is not a question of gathering more evidence about the need for change. It is no longer necessary to prove what damage is being done to the world and human societies, nor to understand where this will lead. It is a question of having the will and wisdom to act.

We believe strongly that this change is possible, that humanity can make the necessary transition, and without great hardship. Rather than fearing change, we hope that human society will learn to embrace it, and have the courage and confidence to build a better world.

— ACKNOWLEDGMENTS —

I WOULD LIKE to thank my wife, Bernice (a.k.a. Mitzi, as well as Those Boys and the Girls, naturally). She is that otter spirit bounding by my side with her Northern-Lights hair, connected with me umbilically to what lies beneath the peat, far beneath the lochs, to whatever dark fundament swirls in that other place we know when we stand on the inland shores of Scotia.
—Graeme Maxton

I THANK MY wife, Marie, for warm support through thirty-five years and for accepting that I am still working days and nights long after normal retirement age. And I thank my colleague through many years climate psychologist Per Espen Stoknes for having succeeded in convincing me that the solution to the world's ills does not lie in doomsday predictions but in highlighting a solution that is attractive (in the short term) in the eyes of the voting majority.
—Jorgen Randers

AS WELL AS thanking our cartoonist, Øystein Runde, both of us would like to thank our colleagues in the Club of Rome, the many members who have offered their help and support, especially the co-presidents, Ernst Ulrich von Weizsäcker and Anders Wijkman. We are also very grateful to those working in the secretariat—Thomas Schauer, Alexander Stefes, Melanie Studer, and Sebastian Forsch—for their input, patience, and wisdom. We thank everyone in the club

for keeping their heads when all around were losing theirs, for knowing that what we said in *The Limits to Growth*, all those years ago, was basically right.
—Graeme Maxton and Jorgen Randers

— NOTES —

CHAPTER 1

1. OECD, *Income Inequality: The Gap between Rich and Poor* (2015). Available at www. oecd.org/economy/income-inequality-9789264246010-en.htm

2. Figures from the U.S. Census. See D. Boyer, "That's Rich: Poverty Level under Obama Breaks 50-Year Record," *Washington Times*, December 7, 2015. Available at www.washingtontimes.com/news/2014/jan/7/obamas-rhetoric-on-fight-ing-poverty-doesnt-match-h/?page=all). Poverty is typically defined as half the median income, though there are usually variations for the number of family members. In the EU as a whole, it is defined as 60% of median income. See also Pew Research Center, www.pewsocialtrends.org/2015/12/09/the-ameri-can-middle-class-is-losing-ground and www.pewsocialtrends.org/2016/05/11/ are-you-in-the-american-middle-class. For other perspectives, see www. feedingamerica.org/hunger-in-america/impact-of-hunger/hunger-and-pov-erty/hunger-and-poverty-fact-sheet.html and www.dailymail.co.uk/news/ article-2233137/New-study-shows-49-7-million-Americans-live-poverty-Census-Bureau-release-adjusted-figures-reveal-struggle-survive.html (both refer to 2012).

3. See Inequalitywatch.eu. Figures come from Eurostat 2010.

4. See www.oxfam.org/en/pressroom/pressreleases/2014-01-20/ rigged-rules-mean-economic-growth-increasingly-winner-takes-all.

5. S. Dransfield, "A Tale of Two Britains: Inequality in the UK" (n.p.: Oxfam, March 17, 2014).

CHAPTER 2

1. See www.investopedia.com/terms/i/invisiblehand.asp.

2. A. Sauvy, "Les conséquences sociales et morales du vieillissement de la population," *Canadian Studies in Population*, 6 (1979), and tharunka.arc.unsw.edu.au/dont-teach-economics-gross-domestic-product-gdp-even-matter.

3. A. Maddison, *The World Economy: A Millennial Perspective* (OECD, 2001), Appendix B, p. 28.

4. In per capita purchasing power parity terms.

5. The full title is *An Inquiry into the Nature and Causes of the Wealth of Nations*.

6. Average rate between 1820 and 1900.

7. He also wanted to reduce staff turnover. Conditions were so bad in his factories that he had to hire more than fifty thousand people each year to staff a factory that needed just fourteen thousand.

8. U.S. Census Bureau Demographic Trends in the 20th Century, 2002. Available at www.census.gov/prod/2002pubs/censr-4.pdf. See also stats.oecd.org/Index.aspx?DataSetCode=POP_PROJ and ourworldindata.org/data/population-growth-vital-statistics/world-population-growth.

9. In 1990 dollar terms this stood at $1.5 trillion.

10. Evidence submitted to the Select Committee on Economic Affairs, House of Lords, London, for the inquiry into *Aspects of the Economics of Climate Change*, by Professor Angus Maddison FBA, February 20, 2005, page 5, Table 2.

11. Ibid.

12. A. Maddison, U.K. Census 2001, and J. Lahmeyer, U.S. Census, 1820, Population Statistics, database at www.populstat.info.

13. This works out to an average of 13.5 hours per person a week in 2001, which makes little sense. This is because it is spread across the entire population, including children and pensioners. With the full-time working population in the U.K. around a third of the total, 700 hours equates to around a 40-hour week for those with a job, much less than they would have worked in the 1820s.

14. As measured in equivalent years of primary education. See Maddison, *Aspects of the Economics of Climate Change*, p. 4, Table 1.

15. Interestingly, the working year at the end of the nineteenth century was longer than it was at the end of the sixteenth century. On average, people in the U.K. worked more than 300 days a year in the late 1860s, compared with 257 days a year in the late 1500s. Source: G. Clark, *Average Earnings and Retail Prices, UK, 1209-2010* (University of California Davis, October 30, 2011), Table 5.

16. See Maddison, *Aspects of the Economics of Climate Change*, Figure 5G.

17. See Health and Benefit Coverage at stateofworkingamerica.org/data.

18. S. Lebergott, "Wages and Working Conditions," *Concise Encyclopedia of Economics* (1984). Available at www.econlib.org/library/Enc1/WagesandWorkingConditions. html. See also S. Lebergott, *The Americans: An Economic Record* (W.W. Norton, 1984).

19. Per dollar of real GNP between 1900 and the end of the 1980s.

20. In 1980, compared to 1900. See also www.gate.cnrs.fr/IMG/pdf/household-revo-lution-2012-07-19.pdf.

21. From 18% to 52% between 1900 and 1980. See C. Lindsay, *A Century of Labour Market Change* (U.K. Office for National Statistics, Labour Market Trends [LMT], 2003) p. 1.

22. H. Shierholz, *The State of Working America* (12th edition) (Ithaca, NY: Cornell University Press, 2012), Figure 2AA.

23. E. Saez, Income Concentration and Top Income Tax Rates, USC Tax Policy.

24. K. Pickett and R. Wilkinson, *The Spirit Level: Why Equality Is Better for Everyone* (London: Penguin, 2010).

CHAPTER 3

1. J.M. Keynes, "Economic Possibilities for Our Grandchildren," in *Essays on Persuasion, Keynes on Possibilities* (1930).

2. All dollar amounts in this book are measured in 2005 PPP (Purchasing Power Parity) U.S. dollars.

3. There is some debate about when this particular crisis actually began, with some economists pointing to the peak of the U.S. housing market in 2006 as the turning point, and others saying that the problems first became serious when banks started calling in their loans in the second half of 2007. Most economists say it started in 2008, however, because this is when the immediate consequences peaked and financial institutions began to collapse.

4. Shierholz, *State of Working America*, Chapter 4, Figure 4D.

5. Shierholz, *State of Working America*, Chapter 4, Table 6N.

6. Shierholz, *State of Working America*, Chapter 4, Figure 4C.

7. Shierholz, *State of Working America*, Chapter 4, Table 4.1.

8. U.S. Bureau of Economic Analysis—figure is compound real growth.

9. From 16.3% to 17.5%.

10. In 2011, the income threshold for a four-person family to classify them as living in poverty was $23,021, according to the U.S. Census Bureau.

11. Shierholz, *State of Working America*, Chapter 7, Chart 7B.

12. P. Gregg, S. Machin, and M. Fernández-Salgado, "Real Wages and Unemployment in the Big Squeeze," *Economic Journal*, 124, 408–32 (2014).

13. IMF Database: www.imf.org/en/Data#global.

14. OECD and Eurostat: stats.oecd.org/index.aspx and ec.europa.eu/eurostat.

15. Shierholz, *State of Working America*.

16. Shierholz, *State of Working America*, Figure 4AK.

17. IMF Database figures for "Advanced economies" in nominal terms. See www.imf.org/en/Data.

18. Shierholz, *State of Working America*, Wealth, Table 60.

19. Shierholz, *State of Working America*, Figure 2AA.

20. OECD Insights Series, *Income Inequality: The Gap between Rich and Poor* (December 15, 2015). See www.oecd.org/insights. See also, OECD, *How Was Life? Global Well-Being since 1820*, October 2, 2014. Available at www.oecd.org/statistics/how-was-life-9789264214262-en.htm.

21. Shierholz, *State of Working America*, Figure 2AB.

22. The term originally comes from Japan, which adopted the policy in the 1990s but later said that it did not work.

23. Bank of England interest rates in the U.K. in 2015 were at their lowest level since the bank was founded in 1694.

24. QE and ultra-low interest rates: McKinsey Global Institute, *Distributional Effects and Risks*, consultant's report, November 2013. Available at www.mckinsey.com/global-themes/employment-and-growth/qe-and-ultra-low-interest-rates-distributional-effects-and-risks. Figures are in constant 2012 USD.

25. McKinsey Global Institute, *Distributional Effects and Risks*. Figures in constant 2013 USD.

CHAPTER 4

1. With thanks to Darrell Doren. RFID stands for radio-frequency identification.

2. You can see this even by looking at China, where employment in the manufacturing sector fell, despite the rise in output between 1990 and 2008. A 70% increase in output led to a 25% fall in the number of employees.

3. E. Schonfeld, "Is Technology Destroying Jobs?" (November 15, 2011). Available at techcrunch.com/2011/11/15/technology-destroying-jobs.

4. "Coming to an Office Near You," *The Economist* (January 18, 2014). Available at www.economist.com/news/leaders/21594298-effect-todays-technology-tomorrows-jobs-will-be-immenseand-no-country-ready.

5. B. Frey and M. A. Osborne. "The Future of Employment: How Susceptible Are Jobs to Computerisation?" (2013). Available at www.oxfordmartin.ox.ac.uk/downloads/academic/The_Future_of_Employment.pdf.

6. See www.independent.co.uk/life-style/gadgets-and-tech/softbank-unveils-pepper-japanese-robot-with-a-heart-will-care-for-the-elderly-and-children-9491819.html and www.good.is/articles/robots-elder-care-pepper-exoskeletons-japan.

7. D. Ricardo, *On The Principles of Political Economy and Taxation*, Chapter 31: On Machinery (n.p., 1817).

8. E. Brynjolfsson and A. McAfee, *The Race Against the Machine* (Digital Frontier Press, 2011) and E. Brynjolfsson and A. McAfee, *The Second Machine Age: Work, Progress and Technologies in a Time of Brilliant Technologies* (New York: WW Norton, 2014).

9. Brynjolfsson and McAfee, *The Race Against the Machine*, p. 56.

CHAPTER 5

1. H.S. Dent Foundation, cited by S. Ro in "35 Amazing Graphs that Show How Your Spending Habits Change with Age, *The Atlantic* (November 26, 2012). Available at www.theatlantic.com/business/archive/2012/11/35-amazing-graphs-that-show-how-your-spending-habits-change-with-age/265575.

2. The 2010 Bundle Report, Spending by Age, published in the U.S., March 2010 (currently unavailable). See also www.infographicsblog.com/2010-bundle-report-how-america-spends-stefanie-posavec/.

3. H.S. Dent Report.

4. E. Seidle, "The Greatest Retirement Crisis in American History," *Forbes* (March 20, 2013). Available at www.forbes.com/sites/edwardsiedle/2013/03/20/the-greatest-retirement-crisis-in-american-history/#583383351b88.

5. National governments who use the euro within the European Union are unable to increase the volume of the currency in circulation themselves, as this is a regional responsibility of the European Central Bank.

CHAPTER 6

1. D.C. Korten, *When Corporations Rule the World* (20th anniversary edition) (third edition) (San Francisco: Berrett-Koehler Publishers, 2015), p. 24.

2. Scale refers to the volume produced. Because of "economies of scale," a company that makes 500,000 cars a year, for example, can make each car more cheaply than one that makes 5,000 cars a year. This is because the fixed and setup costs for manufacturing complex products like cars are generally very high. The bigger the company, the lower the costs per unit, in other words—at least to a certain point. This means that market entrants, such as those in poor countries, cannot compete with bigger established rivals, especially if there is a small local market, because they are unable to develop the necessary scale to become cost competitive.

3. See www.oecd.org/health/Obesity-Update-2014.pdf and, for example, www.oecd.org/pisa/keyfindings/PISA-2012-results-US.pdf.

CHAPTER 7

1. We have taken some liberties here with Bill McKibben's astute observation that "The laws of Congress and the laws of physics have grown increasingly divergent, and the laws of physics are not likely to yield."

2. Our presentation of the climate issue is a summary of the detailed discussion in J. Randers, 2052: *A Global Forecast for the Next Forty Years* (Hartford, VT: Chelsea Green Publishing, 2012) and J. Randers, U. Goluke, F. Wenstop, and S. Wenstop, "A User-Friendly Earth System Model of Low Complexity: The ESCIMO System Mode of Global Warming towards 2100," *Earth System Dynamics* (2016 in press).

3. Sporadically we use the terms global warming and climate change interchangeably, though we acknowledge that we should not. Technically, according to NASA, global warming is "the increase in Earth's average surface temperature due to rising levels of greenhouse gases," and climate change is "a long term change in the Earth's climate, or a region of the Earth." See "What's in a Name? Global Warming vs. Climate Change" at www.nasa.gov/topics/earth/features/climate_by_any_other_name.html.

4. See J. Randers and P. Gilding "The One Degree War Plan," *Journal of Global Responsibility*, 1(1).

5. U.S. Environmental Protection Agency figures. See www3.epa.gov/climatechange/ghgemissions/gases/n2o.html.

6. J. Randers, "How Fast Will China Grow towards 2030? And What about the U.S.? *World Economics* (June 2016).

7. See C. Martin, *On the Edge: The State and Fate of the World's Tropical Rainforests* (Vancouver, BC: Greystone Books, 2015) (Endspiel, *Wie wir das Schicksal der Tropischen Regenwälder noch wenden können* [Oekom Verlag, 2015]).

CHAPTER 8

1. See, for example, www.guttmacher.org/pubs/social-economic-benefits.pdf.

CHAPTER 9

1. See Graph 3. We have tried to use the same source of data to be consistent in our charts and figures, 2005 PPP USD. The 2015 actual GDP per head in the U.S. was $54,000, and in Germany, $47,000. See the IMF database at www.imf.org/external/pubs/ft/weo/2015/02/weodata/index.aspx.

2. U.S. Bureau of Labor statistics, Table A-1, Employment status of the civilian population by sex and age, seasonally adjusted figures for October 2015. See www.bls.gov.

3. U.S. Bureau of Labor statistics, Table 8, Employed and unemployed full- and part-time workers by age, sex, race and ethnicity. See www.bls.gov.

4. For simplicity, this assumes that everyone works a forty-hour week, and that people working part time currently work twenty hours a week.

5. P. Dockrill, "Working Long Hours Is Linked to a Significantly Higher Risk of Stroke" (Science Alert, August 21, 2015). Available at www.sciencealert.com/working-long-hours-is-linked-to-a-significantly-higher-risk-of-stroke.

6. The Geneva Association, Wissenkapital im Lebensbogen, Patrick Liedtke, Zukunftsforum, Munich, September 17–18, 2009, Silver Workers Institute.

7. Social Security Administration Trustees Report, 2011 Table IV. B2 Ratio of covered workers to beneficiaries.

8. PwC report, "Wider Pensions Reform Needed to Tackle Pension Savings Shortfall" (PwC, September 30, 2013). Available at pwc.blogs.com/press_room/2015/09/wider-pensions-reform-needed-to-tackle-pension-savings-shortfall-.html.

9. A. Sapir, "Globalization and the Reform of European Social Models," *JCMS*, 44(2) (2006), 369–90. Available at www.ulb.ac.be/cours/delaet/econo76/docs/sapir. pdf.

10. D. Gilson, "Survival of the Richest," *Mother Jones*, September/October 2014, p. 33.

11. F. Norris, "Corporate Profits Grow and Wages Slide," *New York Times* (April 4, 2014).

12. Average mileage 13,500 a year, and an average of 20 miles to the gallon.

13. McKinsey & Company, "Pathways to a Low-Carbon Future" (McKinsey & Company, 2009).

14. For more on this, see U. Bardi, *Extracted: How the Quest for Mineral Wealth Is Plundering the Planet* (Vermont: Chelsea Green Publishing, 2014).

15. See globalincome.org and J. O'Farrell, "A No Strings Basic Income? If It Works for the Royal Family, It Can Work for All," *The Guardian* (January 7, 2016). Available at www.theguardian.com/commentisfree/2016/jan/07/ basic-income-royal-family-living-wage-economy.

16. See Locke's Second Treatise on Civil Government, chapter 5, Of Property.

17. A. Smith, *Lectures on Justice, Police, Revenue and Arms*, University of Glasgow 1763, Division III, Private Law, section 4, Fourth Way of acquiring property: Succession.

18. F. Jaumotte and C. Osorio Buiton, *Inequality and Labor Market Institutions*, IMF Staff Discussion Note, July 2015. Available at www.imf.org/external/pubs/ft/ sdn/2015/sdn1514.pdf.

19. F. Jaumotte and C. Osorio Buiton, "Power from the People, IMF Finance and Development" (March 2015). Available at www.imf.org/external/pubs/ft/ fandd/2015/03/pdf/jaumotte.pdf.

20. M. Walters and L. Mishel, *How Unions Help All Workers* (Economic Policy Institute, August 26, 2003). Available at www.epi.org/publication/briefingpapers_bp143.

21. Unionized workers receive 26% more vacation and 14% more total paid leave (vacations and holidays). See Walters and Mishel, *How Unions Help All Workers*.

22. An 18% to 28% higher chance. See Walters and Mishel, *How Unions Help All Workers*.

23. A 23% to 54% higher chance. See Walters and Mishel, *How Unions Help All Workers*.

24. See Trade Unions and Political Actors, at http://pubman.mpdl.mpg.de/pubman/ item/escidoc:1234497/component/escidoc:1234496/5_Streeck_und_Hassel_

2003_Trade_Unions.pdf. See also: www.worker-participation.eu/National-Industrial-Relations/Countries/Germany/Trade-Unions.

25. Center for American Progress, "Bargaining for the American Dream: What Unions Do to Mobility" (September 9, 2015). Available at www.americanprogress.org/issues/economy/report/2015/09/09/120558/bargaining-for-the-american-dream.

26. Trans-Pacific Partnership (TPP), Comprehensive Economic and Trade Agreement (CETA), and Transatlantic Trade and Investment Partnership (TTIP).

27. According to the draft agreement. See C. Provost and M. Kennard, "The Obscure Legal Agreement That Lets Corporations Sue Governments," *The Guardian* (June 10, 2015). Available at www.theguardian.com/business/2015/jun/10/obscure-legal-system-lets-corportations-sue-states-ttip-icsid. See also citizen.org/investorcases.

28. The number of children per woman during her reproductive life is the standard measure of human fertility.

29. Take France, for example. See France Diplomatie, "With 2.01 Children per Woman, France Has One of the Highest Fertility Rates in Europe," October 2013. Available at www.diplomatie.gouv.fr/en/french-foreign-policy/economic-diplomacy-foreign-trade/facts-about-france/one-figure-one-fact/article/2-01-the-average-number-of. Also, for a slightly different perspective, see J.V. Last, "Boomsa for the Motherland: The Creative, Absurd, and Ineffective Ways That Countries Try to Boost Their Birthrates," Slate.com (April 25, 2013). Available at www.slate.com/articles/life/family/2013/04/can_a_country_boost_its_low_birth_rate_examples_from_around_the_world.html.

30. 2005 PPP.

31. Trying to avoid the tax by moving abroad would not help much, since society clearly would have to tax the income that is taken out of the country in the same way as the income that was kept in the country. So the rich would have to move not only themselves but also their profit-generating activities abroad, and then spend their income there if they really wanted to avoid the tax. Many very rich people would certainly be tempted, and so all the countries where it is pleasant to live would have to coordinate their taxation policies. This is unlikely to happen, though the OECD countries are trying hard.

32. In Norway, there are around thirty thousand employees in total in benefits administration, the tax authorities, and the central ministries—out of 2.5 million jobs.

CHAPTER 10

1. Western interference (see Asharq Al-Awsat, "Egypt: Compelling Evidence in US NGO Case," Asharq Al-Awsat, February 8, 2012. Available at english.aawsat. com/2012/02/article55243285/egypt-compelling-evidence-in-us-ngo-case-source. See also R. Nixon, "U.S. Groups Helped Nurture Arab Uprisings," *New York Times*, April 14, 2011. Available at www.nytimes.com/2011/04/15/world/15aid. html?_r=4&pagewanted=1&emc=eta1). NGOs played a large part in the Arab Spring of 2011, especially in Egypt, where Western NGOs spent millions of dollars trying to direct the revolution and manipulate the political process (see "Egypt Lifts Travel Ban on Seven US Pro-Democracy Campaigners," *The Guardian*, February 29, 2012. Available at www.theguardian.com/world/2012/feb/29/egypt-travel-ban-us-campaigners). Many of those working for these NGOs were eventually expelled by the Egyptian government. The United Arab Emirates has also expelled three "pro-democracy" European and U.S. NGOs (pomed.org/blog-post/democracy-promotion/u-a-e-authorities-expel-pro-democracy-ngos/), which the government found to be tinkering with the country's internal affairs. After the revolution in Libya (see J. Dettmer, "Libya's Civil Crackdown Worries Democracy Advocates," *The Daily Beast*, May 28, 2012, at www.thedailybeast. com/articles/2012/05/28/exclusive-libya-s-civil-crackdown-worries-democracy-advocates.html), the government there attempted to stop U.S. and European groups funding local NGOs as well. Other countries known to have expelled Westerners for interfering in the democratic process include Russia, Pakistan, North Korea, Syria, Sudan, and Bolivia. Many of the same NGOs that were in North Africa in 2011 also played a part in the changes that took place in Myanmar (see T. Cartalucci, "Globalists Grind Development to a Halt in Myanmar," December 3, 2011; at landdestroyer.blogspot.se/2011/12/fruits-of-globalization-regression. html). There are also reports that Western-backed groups have intervened in the political freedoms of both Thailand (see T. Cartalucci, "Exposed: Indy 'Newspaper' Funded by US Government," August 10, 2011, at landdestroyer.blogspot. se/2011/08/exposed-indy-newspaper-funded-by-us.html) and Malaysia (see, for example, T. Cartalucci, "The 'Democracy' Racket: US Covert Attempt to Implement 'Regime Change' in Malaysia," February 17, 2013, at www.globalresearch.ca/the-democracy-racket-us-covert-attempt-to-implement-regime-change-in-malaysia/5323194, and "US vs China: US-Backed Mobs Seek to Overthrow Malaysian Government," August 24, 2015, at landdestroyer.blogspot.ca/2015/08/us-vs-china-us-mobs-seek-to-overthrow.html).

CHAPTER 11

1. See Transparency International's Corruption Index: www.transparency.org/research/cpi/overview.

2. Global Footprint Network. See www.footprintnetwork.org/en/index.php/GFN/ page/world_footprint.

3. Currently installed energy capacity is around 3 kW for each of the world's 7 billion people.

4. See www.theguardian.com/global-development-professionals-network/2015/ mar/30/it-will-take-100-years-for-the-worlds-poorest-people-to-earn-125-a-day.

5. United Nations Millennium Development Goals Report, July 2015. Available at www.un.org/millenniumgoals/2015_MDG_Report/pdf/MDG%202015%20 rev%20(July%201).pdf.

6. OECD, *How Was Life? Global Well-Being since 1820*, October 2014. Available at www. oecd.org/statistics/how-was-life-9789264214262-en.htm.

7. See www.globalissues.org/article/4/poverty-around-the-world. Chart data taken from World Bank Development Indicators 2008: data.worldbank.org/sites/ default/files/wdi08.pdf.

8. See www.wsws.org/en/articles/2015/04/17/pove-a17.html.

CHAPTER 12

1. D.H. Meadows, D.L. Meadows, J. Randers, and W.W. Behrens III, *The Limits to Growth* (New York: New American Library, 1972). See also www.alternet.org/ story/18978/facing_the_limits_to_growth, June 2004.

2. See Global Footprint Network 2015 report. Available at www.footprintnetwork. org/en/index.php/GFN/page/public_data_package.

3. J. Randers, "Global Collapse—Fact or Fiction?" *Futures*, 40(10), 853-864, December 2008. Available at dx.doi.org10.1016/j.futures.2008.07.042.

4. A. Wijkman and K. Skånberg, *The Circular Economy and Benefits for Society*, study by the Club of Rome, April 2015. Available at www.clubofrome.org/wp-content/ uploads/2016/03/The-Circular-Economy-and-Benefits-for-Society.pdf.

CHAPTER 13

1. S.G. Medema, "The Economic Role of Government in the History of Economic Thought," in W.J. Samuels, J.E. Biddle, and J. B. Davis (eds), *A Companion to the History of Economic Thought* (Malden, MA: Blackwell Publishing Ltd., 2003), chapter 27, pages 234-35. doi: 10.1002/9780470999059.

— SELECT BIBLIOGRAPHY AND — FURTHER READING

Asharq Al-Awsat. (February 8, 2012). "Egypt: Compelling Evidence in US NGO Case." Available at english.aawsat.com/2012/02/article55243285/egypt-compelling-evidence-in-us-ngo-case-source.

Bardi, U. (2014). *Extracted: How the Quest for Mineral Wealth Is Plundering the Planet.* Vermont, Chelsea Green Publishing.

Boyer, D. (January 7, 2014). "That's Rich: Poverty Level under Obama Breaks 50-Year Record. *Washington Times.* Available at www.washingtontimes.com/news/2014/jan/7/obamas-rhetoric-on-fighting-poverty-doesnt-match-h/?page=all.

Brynjolfsson, E., and McAfee, A. (2011). *The Race Against the Machine.* Digital Frontier Press.

Brynjolfsson, E., and McAfee, A. (2014). *The Second Machine Age: Work, Progress and Technologies in a Time of Brilliant Technologies.* New York: WW Norton.

Cardia. E., and Gomme, P. (2011). "The Household Revolution: Childcare, Housework, and Female Labor Force Participation." Université de Montréal and CIREQ; Concordia University and CIREQ. Available at www.gate.cnrs.fr/IMG/pdf/household-revolution-2012-07-19.pdf.

Cartalucci, T. (August 10, 2011). "Exposed: Indy 'Newspaper' Funded by US Government." Available at landdestroyer.blogspot.se/2011/08/exposed-indy-newspaper-funded-by-us.html.

Cartalucci, T. (December 3, 2011). "Globalists Grind Development to a Halt in Myanmar." Available at landdestroyer.blogspot.se/2011/12/fruits-of-globalization-regression.html.

Cartalucci, T. (February 17, 2013). "The 'Democracy' Racket: US Covert Attempt to Implement 'Regime Change' in Malaysia." Available at www.globalresearch.ca/the-democracy-racket-us-covert-attempt-to-implement-regime-change-in-malaysia/5323194.

Cartalucci, T. (August 24, 2015). "US vs China: US-Backed Mobs Seek to Overthrow Malaysian Government." Available at landdestroyer.blogspot.ca/2015/08/us-vs-china-us-mobs-seek-to-overthrow.html.

Center for American Progress. (September 9, 2015). "Bargaining for the American Dream: What Unions Do to Mobility." Available at www.americanprogress.org/issues/economy/report/2015/09/09/120558/bargaining-for-the-american-dream.

Clark, G. (2011). *Average Earnings and Retail Prices, UK, 1209–2010*. University of California, Davis. Available at www.measuringworth.com/datasets/ukearncpi/earnstudynew.pdf.

Dettmer, J. (May 28, 2012). "Libya's Civil Crackdown Worries Democracy Advocates." *The Daily Beast*. Available at www.thedailybeast.com/articles/2012/05/28/exclusive-libya-s-civil-crackdown-worries-democracy-advocates.html.

Dockrill, P. (August 21, 2015). "Working Long Hours Is Linked to a Significantly Higher Risk of Stroke." *Science Alert*. Available at www.sciencealert.com/working-long-hours-is-linked-to-a-significantly-higher-risk-of-stroke.

Dransfield, S. (March 2014). *A Tale of Two Britains: Inequality in the UK*. N.p.: Oxfam GB. Available at policy-practice.oxfam.org.uk/publications/a-tale-of-two-britains-inequality-in-the-uk-314152.

The Economist. (January 18, 2014). "Coming to an Office Near You." Available at www.economist.com/news/leaders/21594298-effect-todays-technology-tomorrows-jobs-will-be-immenseand-no-country-ready.

France Diplomatie. (October 2013). "With 2.01 Children per Woman, France Has One of the Highest Fertility Rates in Europe." Available at www.diplomatie.gouv.fr/en/french-foreign-policy/economic-diplomacy-foreign-trade/facts-about-france/one-figure-one-fact/article/2-01-the-average-number-of.

Frey B., and Osborne, M.A. (2013). "The Future of Employment: How Susceptible Are Jobs to Computerisation?" Available at www.oxfordmartin.ox.ac.uk/downloads/academic/The_Future_of_Employment.pdf.

Fukuyama, F. (1992/2006). *The End of History and the Last Man*. N.p.: Free Press.

Gilson, D. (September/October 2014). "Survival of the Richest." *Mother Jones*. Available at www.motherjones.com/politics/2014/10/charts-income-inequality-recession-survival-richest.

Global Footprint Network. (2015). *Global Footprint Network 2015 Report*. Available at www.footprintnetwork.org/en/index.php/GFN/page/public_data_package.

Gregg, P., Machin, S., and Fernández-Salgado, M. (2014). "Real Wages and Unemployment in the Big Squeeze," *Economic Journal*, 124, 408-32.

The Guardian. (February 29, 2012). "Egypt Lifts Travel Ban on Seven US Pro-Democracy Campaigners." Available at www.theguardian.com/world/2012/feb/29/egypt-travel-ban-us-campaigners.

Jaumotte, F., and Osorio Buiton, C. (March 2015). "Power from the People, IMF Finance and Development." Available at www.imf.org/external/pubs/ft/fandd/2015/03/pdf/jaumotte.pdf.

Jaumotte, F., and Osorio Buiton, C. (July 2015). *Inequality and Labor Market Institutions*. IMF Staff Discussion Note. Available at www.imf.org/external/pubs/ft/sdn/2015/sdn1514.pdf.

Keynes, J.M. (1930). "Economic Possibilities for Our Grandchildren." In *Essays on Persuasion, Keynes on Possibilities*. Available at www.econ.yale.edu/smith/econ116a/keynes1.pdf.

Korten, D.C. (2015). *When Corporations Rule the World* (20th anniversary edition) (third edition). San Francisco: Berrett-Koehler Publishers.

Last, J.V. (April 25, 2013). "Boomsa for the Motherland: The Creative, Absurd, and Ineffective Ways That Countries Try to Boost Their Birthrates." Slate.com. Available at www.slate.com/articles/life/family/2013/04/can_a_country_boost_its_low_birth_rate_examples_from_around_the_world.html.

Lebergott, S. (1984). *The Americans: An Economic Record*. New York: W.W. Norton.

Lebergott, S. (1984). "Wages and Working Conditions," *Concise Encyclopedia of Economics*. Available at www.econlib.org/library/Enc1/WagesandWorkingConditions.html.

Lindsay, C. (2003). *A Century of Labour Market Change*. London: U.K. Office for National Statistics, Labour Market Trends (LMT).

Maddison, A. (2001). *The World Economy: A Millennial Perspective*. Paris: OECD.

Maddison, A. (February 20, 2005). *Aspects of the Economics of Climate Change*. Evidence submitted to the Select Committee on Economic Affairs, House of Lords, London, for the inquiry into Aspects of the Economics of Climate Change. Available at www.publications.parliament.uk/pa/ld200506/ldselect/ldeconaf/12/12i.pdf.

Martin, C. (2015). *On the Edge: The State and Fate of the World's Tropical Rainforests.* Vancouver, BC: Greystone Books. (Endspiel. [2015]. *Wie wir das Schicksal der Tropischen Regenwälder noch wenden können.* Munich: Oekom Verlag.)

Maxton, G. (2011). *The End of Progress.* Wiley Books.

McKinsey & Company. (2009). "Pathways to a Low-Carbon Future." McKinsey & Company.

McKinsey Global Institute. (November 2013). *Distributional Effects and Risks.* (Consultant's report.) Available at www.mckinsey.com/global-themes/ employment-and-growth/qe-and-ultra-low-interest-rates-distributional-effects-and-risks.

Meadows, D.H., Meadows, D. L., Randers, J., and Behrens III, W.W. (1972). *The Limits to Growth.* New York: New American Library.

Nixon, R. (April 14, 2011). "U.S. Groups Helped Nurture Arab Uprisings." *New York Times.* Available at www.nytimes.com/2011/04/15/world/15aid. html?_r=4&pagewanted=1&emc=eta1.

Norris, F. (April 4, 2014). "Corporate Profits Grow and Wages Slide." *New York Times.* Available at www.nytimes.com/2014/04/05/business/economy/corporate-profits-grow-ever-larger-as-slice-of-economy-as-wages-slide.html?_r=0.

O'Farrell, J. (January 7, 2016). "A No Strings Basic Income? If It Works for the Royal Family, It Can Work for All." *The Guardian.* Available at www.theguardian.com/ commentisfree/2016/jan/07/basic-income-royal-family-living-wage-economy.

OECD. (June 2014). *Obesity Update.* Available at www.oecd.org/health/Obesity-Update-2014.pdf.

OECD. (October 2014). *How Was Life? Global Well-Being since 1820.* Available at www. oecd.org/statistics/how-was-life-9789264214262-en.htm.

OECD. (December 15, 2015). *Income Inequality: The Gap between Rich and Poor.* OECD Insights Series. Available at www.oecd.org/insights.

Oxfam. (January 2014). "Working for the Few: Political Capture and Economic Inequality." N.p.: Oxfam International. Available at www.ipu.org/splz-e/unga14/ oxfam.pdf.

Pew Research Center. (December 2015.) "The American Middle Class Is Losing Ground." Available at www.pewsocialtrends.org/2015/12/09/the-american-middle-class-is-losing-ground.

Pew Research Center. (December 2015). "Are You Middle Class?" Available at www. pewsocialtrends.org/2015/12/09/are-you-in-the-american-middle-class.

Pickett K., and Wilkinson, R. (2010). *The Spirit Level: Why Equality Is Better for Everyone*. London: Penguin.

Piketty, T. (2014). *Capital in the Twenty-First Century*. Cambridge, MA: Belknap Press.

Provost, C., and Kennard, M. (June 10, 2015). "The Obscure Legal Agreement that Lets Corporations Sue Governments." *The Guardian*. Available at www. theguardian.com/business/2015/jun/10/obscure-legal-system-lets-corportations-sue-states-ttip-icsid.

Randers, J. (December 2008). "Global Collapse—Fact or Fiction?" *Futures, 40*(10), 853–64. Available at dx.doi.org10.1016/j.futures.2008.07.042.

Randers, J. (2012). *2052: A Global Forecast for the Next Forty Years*. Hartford, VT: Chelsea Green Publishing.

Randers, J., and Gilding, P. (2010). "The One Degree War Plan." *Journal of Global Responsibility, 1*(1).

Randers, J., Goluke, U., Wenstop, F., and Wenstop, S. (2016, in press). "A User-Friendly Earth System Model of Low Complexity: The ESCIMO System Mode of Global Warming towards 2100." *Earth System Dynamics*.

Ricardo, D. (1817). *On the Principles of Political Economy and Taxation*. Available at www.econlib.org/library/Ricardo/ricP.html.

Ro, S. (November 26, 2012). "35 Amazing Graphs that Show How Your Spending Habits Change with Age." *The Atlantic*. Available at www.theatlantic.com/business/archive/2012/11/35-amazing-graphs-that-show-how-your-spending-habits-change-with-age/265575.

Samuels, W.J., Biddle, J.E., and Davis, J.B. (eds). (2003). *A Companion to the History of Economic Thought*. Malden, MA: Blackwell Publishing Ltd.

Sapir, A. (2006). "Globalization and the Reform of European Social Models." *JCMS, 44*(2), 369–90. Available at www.ulb.ac.be/cours/delaet/econo76/docs/sapir.pdf.

Sauvy, A. (1979). "Les conséquences sociales et morales du vieillissement de la population." *Canadian Studies in Population, 6*.

Schonfeld, E. (November 15, 2011). "Is Technology Destroying Jobs?" Available at techcrunch.com/2011/11/15/technology-destroying-jobs.

Seidle, E. (March 20, 2013). "The Greatest Retirement Crisis in American History." *Forbes*. Available at www.forbes.com/sites/edwardsiedle/2013/03/20/the-greatest-retirement-crisis-in-american-history/.

Shierholz, H. (2012). *The State of Working America* (12th edition). Ithaca, NY: Cornell University Press.

Silver, A. (March 17, 2006). "Soft Power: Democracy-Promotion and U.S. NGOs." Council on Foreign Relations. Available at www.cfr.org/democratization/ soft-power-democracy-promotion-us-ngos/p10164.

Smith, A. (1763). *Lectures on Justice, Police, Revenue and Arms.* Glasgow, U.K.: University of Glasgow. Available at oll.libertyfund.org/titles/2621.

Smith, A. (1776). *An Inquiry into the Nature and Causes of the Wealth of Nations.* Available at www.econlib.org/library/Smith/smWN.html.

United Nations. (2015). *United Nations Millennium Development Goals Report, July 2015.* Available at www.un.org/millenniumgoals/2015_MDG_Report/pdf/MDG%20 2015%20rev%20(July%201).pdf.

Walters, M. and Mishel, L. (August 26, 2003). *How Unions Help All Workers.* Economic Policy Institute. Available at www.epi.org/publication/briefingpapers_bp143.

Wijkman, A., and Skånberg, K. (April 2015). *The Circular Economy and Benefits for Society.* Study by the Club of Rome. Available at www.clubofrome.org/wp-content/ uploads/2016/03/The-Circular-Economy-and-Benefits-for-Society.pdf.

OTHER WEBSITES AND ONLINE ARTICLES OF INTEREST

2008 World Development Indicators, World Bank, data.worldbank.org/sites/default/ files/wdi08.pdf

Eurostat, ec.europa.eu/eurostat

"Facing the Limits to Growth," Alternet, www.alternet.org/story/18978/ facing_the_limits_to_growth

Global Issues, www.globalissues.org/article/4/poverty-around-the-world

Gobal Research, www.globalresearch.ca/the-democracy-racket-us-covert-at- tempt-to-implement-regime-change-in-malaysia/5323194

Inequality Watch, inequalitywatch.eu

Land Destroyer Report, landdestroyer.blogspot.ch/2015/08/us-vs-china-us-mobs- seek-to-overthrow.html

OECD.Stat, stats.oecd.org/index.aspx

Politaia, www.politaia.org/globalisierung/malaysia-im-fadenkreuz-des-us- imperialismus

Population Statistics, www.populstat.info

State of Working America, stateofworkingamerica.org/data

Tharunka, tharunka.arc.unsw.edu.au/dont-teach-economics-gross-domestic-product-gdp-even-matter

World Socialist Web Site, www.wsws.org/en/articles/2015/04/17/pove-a17.html

GRAEME MAXTON is the secretary general of the Club of Rome and the author of *The End of Progress: How Modern Economics Has Failed Us*. He lives in Zurich, Switzerland.

JORGEN RANDERS is one of the co-authors of the best-selling 1972 book *The Limits to Growth* and author of the 2012 book *2052: A Global Forecast for the Next Forty Years*. He was formerly the president of, and is currently professor emeritus in climate strategy at, the BI Norwegian Business School. He was deputy director general of WWF International and chaired the commission that showed how Norway can reduce its greenhouse gas emissions by 60% by 2050. He lives in Oslo, Norway.

ØYSTEIN RUNDE is an award-winning Norwegian cartoonist. His novel about the Viking Sleggja is currently being turned into a movie.

Graphs and tables are indicated by page numbers in italics

— ABOUT THE CLUB OF ROME —

FORMED IN 1968, the Club of Rome comprises around 100 notable scientists, economists, businessmen, high-level civil servants, and former heads of state from around the world. Its mission is to promote understanding of the long-term challenges facing humanity and to propose holistic solutions through scientific analysis, communication, and advocacy. Part of the Club's work involves the accreditation of a limited number of peer-reviewed reports, the most famous of which is *The Limits to Growth*, which was published in 1972. To be considered as a Report to the Club of Rome, a publication must be innovative, present new approaches, and provide intellectual progress, as compared to other publications on the same topic. It must be based on sound scientific analysis and have a theme that fits the priorities of the Club. *Reinventing Prosperity* is the latest such report.

DAVID
SUZUKI
INSTITUTE

THE DAVID SUZUKI Institute is a nonprofit organization founded in 2010 to stimulate debate and action on environmental issues. The institute and the David Suzuki Foundation both work to advance awareness of environmental issues important to all Canadians.

We invite you to support the activities of the institute. For more information please contact us at:

David Suzuki Institute
219–2211 West 4th Avenue
Vancouver, BC, Canada V6K 4S2
info@davidsuzukiinstitute.org
604-742-2899
www.davidsuzukiinstitute.org

Cheques can be made payable to the David Suzuki Institute.